ONE GOAL

The Mindset of Winning Soccer Teams

Bill Beswick

Human Kinetics

Library of Congress Cataloging-in-Publication Data

Beswick, Bill.
One goal : the mindset of winning soccer teams / Bill Beswick.
   pages cm
Includes bibliographical references and index.
1. Soccer--Psychological aspects. I. Title.
GV943.9.P7B477 2016
796.334019--dc23

                          2015015769

ISBN: 978-1-4504-6578-6 (print)

The web addresses cited in this text were current as of June 2015, unless otherwise noted.

Acquisitions Editor: Chris Wright; **Managing Editor:** Elizabeth Evans; **Copyeditor:** Bob Replinger; **Indexer:** Laurel Plotzke; **Permissions Manager:** Martha Gullo; **Graphic Designer:** Angela K. Snyder; **Cover Designer:** Jonathan Kay; **Photograph (cover):** AP Photo/Matthias Schrader; **Photographs (interior):** © Human Kinetics, unless otherwise noted; **Photo Asset Manager:** Laura Fitch; **Visual Production Assistant:** Joyce Brumfield; **Photo Production Manager:** Jason Allen; **Art Manager:** Kelly Hendren; **Associate Art Manager:** Alan L. Wilborn; **Illustrations:** © Human Kinetics, unless otherwise noted; **Printer:** Sheridan Books

Human Kinetics books are available at special discounts for bulk purchase. Special editions or book excerpts can also be created to specification. For details, contact the Special Sales Manager at Human Kinetics.

Printed in the United States of America

10 9 8 7 6 5 4 3 2 1

The paper in this book is certified under a sustainable forestry program.

Human Kinetics

Website: www.HumanKinetics.com

United States: Human Kinetics
P.O. Box 5076
Champaign, IL 61825-5076
800-747-4457
e-mail: humank@hkusa.com

Canada: Human Kinetics
475 Devonshire Road Unit 100
Windsor, ON N8Y 2L5
800-465-7301 (in Canada only)
e-mail: info@hkcanada.com

Europe: Human Kinetics
107 Bradford Road
Stanningley
Leeds LS28 6AT, United Kingdom
+44 (0) 113 255 5665
e-mail: hk@hkeurope.com

Australia: Human Kinetics
57A Price Avenue
Lower Mitcham, South Australia 5062
08 8372 0999
e-mail: info@hkaustralia.com

New Zealand: Human Kinetics
P.O. Box 80
Mitcham Shopping Centre, South Australia 5062
0800 222 062
e-mail: info@hknewzealand.com

E6062

PRAISE FOR *ONE GOAL*

"This inspirational new release offers insightful ideas from the very highest level of sport. Bill Beswick's influence with countless winning teams makes *One Goal* a top priority for anyone seeking to become the best in sport, business and life."

Tom Bates
Performance Psychologist, West Bromwich Albion Football Club

"The lessons I have learned from my mentor can now be yours. Read *One Goal* and become a better coach."

Steve Round
Former Assistant Manager, Manchester United, Everton

"For nearly 20 years, Bill Beswick has given me great advice at the college and MLS levels. He has helped me become a better coach and, more important, a better person. I cannot recommend his work more highly."

Schellas Hyndman
Head Men's Soccer Coach, Grand Canyon University

"I value Bill Beswick's wisdom in helping our team work toward achieving their potential each year. His understanding of situations and individuals makes him an amazing resource for all coaches."

Shelley Smith
Head Women's Soccer Coach, University of South Carolina

"Bill Beswick has built my awareness of the importance of a team mindset. Learn how to keep your team relationships healthy with *One Goal*."

Anthony Hudson
Head Coach, New Zealand National Team

"Meeting with Bill is best, but this book is a good second best. It has a special place on my desk so I can continue to help in developing the stars of tomorrow."

Chris Panayiotou
Developmental Director of Coaching, Virginia Rush Soccer Club

CONTENTS

FOREWORD

I have been fortunate enough to have had a playing career of 18 years with two great clubs, Manchester United and Everton, and to have represented my country in the England National Team. As one of the 'Class of 92' at United I was part of a team that achieved everything it's possible to achieve in football. The emphasis under the leadership of Sir Alex Ferguson was on winning as a team. Though we had many star individual players, the team always came first. Our strength as a team meant that in the closing stages of games our togetherness and mental resilience would dominate.

When I moved to Everton I took the lessons from United with me. The manager, David Moyes, encouraged me to lead and soon made me captain. Fortunately David and Everton believed in a 'team first' approach, and I was able to strengthen this mindset both on and off the field. Whilst not winning major trophies, Everton consistently stayed in the top eight of the Premier League and qualified to compete in Europe in several seasons. Though considered as having less talent than United, Everton built a similarly tough winning mindset, based on professionalism, dedication and resilience. As captain I understood and relished my responsibility as a leader to shape the team's thinking.

Now that I'm taking my coaching qualifications I often reflect on how that winning team mindset at United and Everton was created and maintained. That's why I was pleased to find that Bill had written this book on the topic to help the next generation of coaches. Bill and I have often spoken together, so I know he understands what makes players and teams tick. That's why I can recommend this book to other coaches keen to develop their teams.

Phil Neville
Manchester United
Everton
England

PREFACE

This book reflects my long experience with teams at grassroots, professional and international levels. Its purpose is to share a key lesson learned: that teams win not only because they have superior talent but also because they have a superior mindset.

Team mindset—the way that a team collectively think and feel in any given situation—is a powerful weapon that governs winning behaviour when positive, focused and strong. Many teams with lesser talent have won because of the strength of their attitude. Likewise, talented teams with weaker mindsets are always vulnerable to shock defeats. Of course, great talent plus great mindset is an unbeatable combination.

My role is to help coaches build a winning mindset in their team. In the competitive world of soccer, this is an everyday challenge. Team mindset is always under pressure from a wide range of negative influences. Coaches may find themselves injecting confidence when their team are anxious and adding a measure of anxiety when their team are too confident.

This need to build a positive team mindset applies to all coaches and all teams regardless of age, gender or level of competition. Teams can only maximise on their talent if they have a mindset fully committed to the hard work of preparing to win. Winning teams are characterised by their passion to practice and learn and their toughness to persist regardless of circumstances.

This book is written in the language of coaches and players, and it is intended to stimulate and help readers. It is organised into three sections that build upon each other in sequence. With a concept like mindset, however, many of the issues described throughout the book are interrelated, so I have deliberately reinforced some important points from chapter to chapter. Some readers will want to dip into the chapters that strike them as particularly relevant; others will enjoy a cover-to-cover read.

Part I, 'Direction' (chapters 1 through 4), lays the foundation for a team mindset built on unity of purpose and direction. In these four initial chapters the primary importance of getting everyone, both in and around the team, on the same page is emphasised, as are the benefits of creating a positive environment that encourages and supports a fighter mentality. Examining the mental strength to deal with the challenges of competition and exploring the extra impetus provided by the right player leadership are covered in chapters 3 and 4. Overall, part I gives readers a solid platform from which to develop greater understanding of how to develop a winning team mindset.

Part II, 'Relationships' (chapters 5 through 9), focuses on the power released when players are treated as human beings as they work on perfecting the tasks they undertake—their 'human doings'. The first of these five chapters looks at how building positive team relationships leads to the extra emotional power of a team playing for one another, not just with each other. Modern soccer increasingly requires players who are intelligent and remain open to new learning experiences, covered in chapter 6, 'Fostering Coachability', and who are sufficiently mature to be held accountable for their play, the theme of chapter 7. The value of merging individual abilities and attitudes into a synchronised team who can execute seamlessly is the subject of chapter 8. Finally, chapter 9 opens discussion on the vital ever-present challenge for coaches—managing team mood through what is often a long, hard season.

The final section, part III, 'Performance' (chapters 10 through 15), moves on to team mindset in action, covering ways in which mindset can be developed to minimise barriers to team play and assist in achieving winning performances. Topics covered in these chapters include competing cohesively, understanding and influencing game momentum, in chapters 10 and 11, and dealing with the negative threats of pressure and adversity, in chapters 12 and 13, respectively. Chapter 14 then examines the issue of keeping a team fresh and full of energy, despite the rigours of a long season, a key factor in end-of-season success when playoffs and decisive league positions loom! Finally, even winning can bring its own mindset problems. Chapter 15 looks at strategies that help coaches and players sustain excellence with continued success.

This whole, complex area of team mindset is one that coaches frequently question me about. Therefore, I have become more involved and interested in increasing my own knowledge and sharing relevant experience. So although this book obviously draws examples mainly from soccer, each chapter is illustrated by a wide range of stories, quotations and references from other team sports and great coaches. One universal characteristic of coaches who desire to improve themselves and their athletes is being open to learning, receiving new ideas and absorbing other experiences to assimilate into their own developing philosophies. Therefore, I make no apologies for the wide range of references. Instead, I sincerely hope that aspiring coaches and athletes will find them stimulating and helpful in understanding how soccer excellence is created. My hope is that this book will help coaches at all levels understand how mindset can be a weapon to win, what can create or destroy it and what they can do to nurture it.

The good news is that mindset is a choice. This book provides many examples of players and teams who improve their performance from the moment they elect to change their mindset from negative to positive. Coaches are a prime influence. Throughout this book they will find a range of practical strategies that they can apply to ensure that their team make choices that lead towards a winning mindset.

This process is not easy. Shaping mindsets individually and collectively takes dedication, concentration and repetition. Development must take place alongside the training of physical skills because the two are interdependent. The mindset of the team governs its readiness to perform, whereas physiological arousal governs the intensity of effort. A team cannot perform the same amount of work or reach the same level of quality under a negative mindset compared with what they can achieve when positive.

The task of coaches reading this book is to interpret the messages, stories and illustrations that are pertinent to their situation and use them in a manner that relates specifically to their own team context. To that end I encourage coaches to see themselves as a little more of a psychologist and a little less of a trainer. I guarantee that they and their team will enjoy and benefit from the change.

Bill Beswick
2015

ACKNOWLEDGMENTS

The coach is a gatekeeper to their players, and over the years I have been fortunate enough to meet a number of far-sighted soccer coaches who have allowed me to work closely with them and engage with their teams. Steve McClaren, Mike Noonan and Schellas Hyndman together with Shelley Smith stand tall among the group, including Mick Wadsworth, Jim Smith, Sir Alex Ferguson, Roy Keane and Brent Erwin. They all have my thanks for helping me build the knowledge and experience shared in this book.

Equally valuable is my work with coaches in other team sports. These coaches have helped me shape and confirm many of the underlying principles of team performance and sharpened my belief that the key driver of athletic performance is mindset. So my thanks go also to a remarkable group, including coaches, (and the athletes in their teams), from rugby, basketball and swimming.

This book would not have been written but for the efforts and resilience of my wife Val. Whilst I had the fun of recreating my life in soccer, Val took responsibility for all the hard parts of putting a book together and deserves my heartfelt thanks.

Along with Val, I must thank Chris Wright and Liz Evans from Human Kinetics for steering the way to a better book, and Val Holmes at the Sportsmind office for both her expertise and much needed humour.

Part I

DIRECTION

A winning team mindset begins
when all members of a
team agree to be led in
the same direction.

© WENN.com/age fotostock

Chapter 1

UNIFYING PURPOSE

The challenge of working with teams as compared with individual athletes is the everyday test of keeping a squad of players on the same page and heading in the same direction. A group of players become a team only when they all agree to

- support a common vision and purpose,
- think 'we' before 'me',
- encourage and support each other and
- take responsibility for their particular roles.

A characteristic of the successful soccer teams I have worked with is a simplicity and clarity of message. Good coaches agree with their teams that this is where we want to go, this is how we are going to do it, and this is the role that each of us has to play.

Coaches get in the way of their team when they confuse or keep changing their vision and plan for the team.

The stronger and more compelling that shared vision of success is, the more committed the team become and the more willing they are to set aside personal agendas. The prize worthwhile for the team has to be bigger than the personal interests of the players. After the team have agreed a shared vision, every player should have purpose, a role to play and proper membership of the team.

The initial task of a coach is to establish the clarity of purpose. The team and the staff must share a picture of what they could achieve by working together. The second and more demanding task is to maintain that unifying vision through the emotional highs and lows of a long season. I often have to remind coaches that players, especially younger players, easily forget the big picture and then lose track of purpose and progress. A short but effective reminder a couple of times during the season can regenerate enthusiasm and energy.

> I never put names on the back of jerseys—if your priority is your team rather than yourself, what else do you need?
>
> Lou Holtz (1999)
> American football coach

The older the players are, the more important it is that their unifying vision is agreed together. A coach has to excite players with the possibilities that exist for achievement as a team, although such power passes to the team only when the players buy in to the idea. A shared vision is especially powerful in women's soccer in which a collective mindset that everyone is comfortable with is a strong driver of motivation and effort. Jon Gordon (2007, p 30) links vision and power: 'Because every journey and ride begins with a desire to go somewhere and do something and if you have a desire then you also have the power to make it happen'.

Coaches often need help when they take over an underachieving team. In their enthusiasm they easily make the mistake of trying to reshape performance without first reshaping attitude. The process I recommend is first about establishing and agreeing about *why* (the cause), then about *how* (the approach to be taken) and finally about *what* (the tasks that both coaches and players have to undertake). Fuelled with a common, unifying purpose, the players change their attitude and improved performance follows. The trick is to excite, engage, enthuse and capture the energy and smartness of the players and channel that toward the unifying vision. Many coaches have yet to appreciate the power of a fully unified, cohesive team.

Setting Goals

Teams need to feel that the journey of preparation and playing they take together could result in something worthwhile and significant. This dream switches on enthusiasm and energy. But this big picture can get lost in the course of a demanding season. So teams need the big ambitions broken down into realistic and attainable goals that they can focus on every practice and game. Saying, 'We want to win the championship' at the start of the season is not enough. Coaches also have to remind their teams to identify and emphasise what they need to do every time they meet to make championship success happen. Nothing characterises a great team more than their sense of purpose and direction at practice times. Goal-setting produces

- a sense of focus and direction,
- a sense of purpose, excitement, energy,
- understandable targets—difficult but realistic,
- a feeling of being in control,
- a momentum to improve continually,
- a sense of urgency, because goals can be time set, and
- a sense of importance, because goals can be measured.

The former manager of Manchester United, Sir Alex Ferguson, was clear on two key goals for his team:

1. Never lose two games in a row. This standard breeds mental toughness and resilience.
2. Always get the second goal. One goal gives you a chance; the second nearly always seals the win.

Undertaking a start-of-season goal-setting exercise with FC Twente, a leading soccer team in Holland, I started first-team players and coaches with some key questions: Do you want to be last year's team? Do you want to be last year's players?

This approach allowed me to emphasise that a new season is a clean sheet and an opportunity to go somewhere new and better. Now was the time for the team to decide on the goals they felt they could, should and must agree. The higher the level and the more senior the team are, the more important it is that goal setting is a shared exercise in which players discuss, agree and take ownership of team and individual goals. For this exercise with FC Twente, the squad and coaches were split into four groups—goalkeepers, defenders, midfielders and attackers. They completed three exercises.

Exercise 1

- Each group brainstormed the possible goals for their position.
- They agreed the five most important goals.
- They reported back to the whole squad.

Exercise 2

- Each group agreed their goals as a unit (e.g., defenders).
- They reported back on key unit goals for the season.

Exercise 3

- Each group agreed six goals for the whole team.
- Each group reported back.
- The whole squad decided the six team goals that had the most support.

With the exercises completed, the then head coach, Steve McClaren, reviewed the goals and described the kind of players and team that the agreed goals would demand. He then talked about what would have to happen to meet the goals. As an important follow-up reminder, the goals agreed were set into a poster that was displayed in the clubhouse and team locker-room.

FC Twente won the first six games of the season and led the league by Christmas. The setting of tough yet attainable goals agreed by all players can provide a powerful boost to performance.

Therefore, coaches need to establish a few key outcome goals: what is to be achieved and more performance and process goals, and what has to be done to achieve them. Setting team goals should follow a plan similar to the following steps:

1. Decide what you want to achieve and why.
2. Write it down.
3. Set deadlines.
4. Make an action plan.
5. List obstacles and difficulties.
6. Prioritise time and energy.
7. Establish mileposts.
8. Measure progress.
9. Succeed and celebrate!

Creating a Team Identity

After teams are bound together by a unifying purpose and agreed set of goals, the next question to be answered is, 'What kind of team do we want to be?' Under pressure to produce results, coaches often ignore this question, but developing a clear and strong team identity is the start to a clear, strong and consistent performance on the field. At the start of each season there is great value in discussing with the team how they want to prepare and play and how they would like others to describe them.

When working with the England senior men's soccer team, I became concerned at the lack of a clear, cohesive team identity. Players from several club teams were asked to come together with little preparation and produce excellent soccer without the glue of an agreed team identity and personality. To begin the process, I asked the squad to describe the kind of team Manchester United was. After establishing some key words, we then repeated the exercise for Liverpool, Chelsea and Arsenal. The players were comfortable with this exercise and confident in their answers.

The players were much less certain in their thoughts when I moved on to the England team. There was some confusion about team identity, and emotional connection was lacking. This lack of clarity was an obstacle to performance as a team, and the coaches and I immediately began a programme with the players to build a stronger team identity.

Team Culture

Culture, the way in which things get done and what the team stand for, shapes team mindset. In a successful team the unifying purpose is reflected and reinforced every day by the underpinning culture and values system.

Purpose—this is what we are going to do.

Culture—this is the way this team will approach the task.

Values—these are the standards we will set.

Teams with a successful culture and values system generally have players and staff that really want to be at practice and games and perform to the best of their ability. The most telling sign of decline at a soccer club is a loss of joy and purpose in practicing and playing soccer. Participants become victims, not volunteers!

A coach needs to answer three vital questions to develop successful team culture:

1. What behaviour, on and off the field, do we want at this club? Now, soon, in the longer term?

2. Who (players and staff already here) is giving us that behaviour? How do we ensure that future players and staff will behave the way we want?

3. What aspects of our coaching and playing situation act in support (or as a barrier) to the behaviour we want?

Establishing a successful, modern soccer culture means putting players at the centre of the operation (see figure 1.1), sharing ownership of the team and shaping winning behaviours by caring for players as people first and then helping them become better soccer players. Such clubs achieve a healthy balance of people care and performance. Feedback such as the following from the players always reinforces this.

- This club cares about me.
- I am important, and I feel good.
- I want to play well and win for these guys.
- We all work out problems together.
- I have fewer problems with my nonsoccer life here.
- There seems to be less stress here.
- I don't want to change clubs.

The 'E' Culture

Great **E**ffort

Great **E**nthusiasm

Great **E**xecution

Great **E**ndurance

However good the purpose and process of practice is, the players and their passion to achieve drive the programme and deliver the performance. When coaches

> ## Figure 1.1　Putting Players First: A Coach's Checklist
>
> - It's about the players—not you.
> - Think from a player's point of view.
> - Use names and build relationships.
> - Plan a player-centred programme.
> - Emphasise the purpose of the work every session.
> - Where possible, share ownership with players.
> - See what players can do, not what they can't do.
> - Become a 'belief partner' to players.
> - Focus on production but allow fun!
> - Balance work, rest and relaxation.

ignore their players as people, those players will start to ignore the coach's demands for excellence—losing motivation, discipline and quality whilst finding excuses, blaming and discovering minor injuries. Coaches should follow the advice of Ralph Waldo Emerson: 'Trust men and they will be true to you. Treat them greatly and they will show themselves great'.

This quotation reminds me of when Middlesbrough FC, struggling with injuries, considered playing a 17-year-old Lee Cattermole in central midfield against a strong Newcastle team at their home stadium, St James' Park. One by one the staff ruled Lee out as an option until Coach Steve Round declared in strong terms that Lee was ready and could be trusted. In a truly remarkable performance, Lee was voted game MVP. This shows that young players are unlikely to develop their talent fully unless they have the benefit of a coach who acts as a belief partner and trusts in their ability to perform at a higher level. Lee Cattermole has gone on to have an excellent career in the Premier League, including captaincy of Sunderland FC.

Team Values

An important element of a successful team culture is establishing a set of shared values. A team's values and beliefs shape both mindset and behaviour. They give each player and the team a framework for dealing with themselves, others and soccer situations. They underpin everything a team does and ensure that the individuals become not only better players but also better people.

A values-driven team can also generate the power and discipline needed to become winners. Many coaches are beginning to understand

© Terry Wild Stock

A strong team has shared values that bring them together.

that team success requires both talent and character and that a strong, competitive character emerges from a sound value system.

Arguably the most successful team in international sport, the New Zealand All-Blacks rugby team, clean their own locker-room after the game, showing the humility that is common to many great teams.

> While the country is still watching replays and school kids lie in bed dreaming of All-Black glory, the All-Blacks themselves are tidying up after themselves.
>
> Sweeping up the sheds (locker-rooms)
>
> Doing it properly
>
> So no one else has to
>
> Because no one looks after the All-Blacks,
>
> The All-Blacks look after themselves. (Kerr 2013, p 7)

This example from another team sport points at a growing problem in youth soccer where rewards are expected, and often given, before they are earned. Whilst other sports, such as the previous rugby example, are building character and values by emphasising effort, commitment and responsibility in the process of becoming excellent, soccer is in danger of overemphasising results and devaluing character development. As a consequence, many promising young players fail to make senior teams through a lack of character and resilience.

Coaches can help to mould team values through a three-step process.

Step 1. Agree on the values that the team wishes to be known by, such as humility, self-discipline, selflessness, courage, unity, passion, dedication, resilience, integrity and so on.

Step 2. Decide what these values mean in action, linking each value with appropriate behaviour on and off the soccer field.

Step 3. Reflect these values in all team processes: recruiting, work ethic, practice and game conduct, dealing with victory or defeat and so on.

Head men's soccer coach Mike Noonan at Clemson University centres his coaching philosophy and style on a unifying set of values agreed by all his players and staff in preseason discussions. On the locker-room wall an impressive poster lists the expectations.

- Do things the right way.
- Pursue excellence in all things.
- Seize the educational opportunity.
- Take the opportunity to be a leader.
- Be a good team member.
- Show maturity and responsibility.
- Give back to your community.
- Have fun—enjoy the soccer experience.

Coach Noonan, his assistants and the team live these values. When several of his key players did not live up to the agreed values, Coach Noonan suspended them for a major game. Even under pressure, he stayed true to the team value system. The suspended players received a character lesson, and the rest of the squad stepped up to win 2-1. This example provides clear evidence of character in action.

Engaging the Players

We have now made the case for coaches to create a unified team mindset by agreeing with their players a powerful and compelling vision for the team's future. This agreement is then made more meaningful and manageable by breaking it down into a number of specific and measurable goals. The whole process is then reinforced by a supportive team culture and value system.

However, such visions, purpose and culture are transformed into winning performance only by players and teams that care about them. Every coach of teams at whatever level, age or gender needs to create the conditions where their players care and commit to the team's unifying purpose.

> I have always felt that every football team I coached would be outstanding if only enough people on the team genuinely cared about our success.
>
> Lou Holtz (1999)
> American football coach

Coaches have to focus on the process of engaging their players in the process of learning soccer by switching on their motivation and willingness to persist. When players are not engaged, the commitment and work rate of the team are likely to be low.

Of course, many players instinctively love the game, but some need inspiration and help in answering the key motivation question, Why? Coaches must be inspirational, sell the benefits and constantly explain why they are asking players to work on particular skills. Coaches have to show players the benefits of their commitment and work.

Most soccer coaches understand that performance follows attitude, in both games and practice. When I visited FC Dallas, I noticed that Coach Schellas Hyndman started practice every day in the locker-room. By taking a few minutes to take the players through the practice session and emphasise the potential benefits for them, Coach Hyndman ensured that his players were engaged. When he sensed the squad were switched on, he moved quickly onto the field. Those few minutes raised the level of motivation and enjoyment of the players and therefore the quality of practice.

Player Centred

The process of coaching must begin by focusing on the person, not the performance. The modern generation of players can pose many problems for coaches. An indulgent upbringing that includes neither responsibility nor challenge can make a player totally unprepared for the demands of a team game or the discipline of a coach. Coaches must develop a relationship with each player that includes knowing names, background and

---

'The Bricks' Pregame Speech

Stuart Lancaster had coached a young England rugby team to the final of the Churchill Cup. Thinking that they needed a pre-game inspirational boost to engage them fully, he delivered the following message.

> Winning is built brick by brick.
> Brick 1 was deciding our sense of purpose—to win this Cup.
> Brick 2 was getting our attitude and commitment right.
> Brick 3 was adding your personal goals.
> Brick 4 was getting our physical condition perfect.
> Brick 5 was sharpening our skills.
> Brick 6 was deciding our game plan.
> Brick 7 was winning and getting to the final.
> Now it is time for the final brick—winning the cup.
> Brick 8 is all about you taking responsibility.
> I trust you to add the final brick!

Simple, short, powerful, engaging and inspirational. The team won. Mission completed.

---

general interests. After relationships have been initiated, coaches must then focus on the process of learning rather than game results. Fear of losing heightens stress and disappointment. But if players are focused on getting better, they will be happier and persist longer.

Given that players love activity, their enthusiasm and involvement rarely breaks down. In general, when it does happen, the cause is one of the following:

- An abusive coach
- Poor organisation and poor practice
- Lack of teaching
- Lack of relationships
- Overinvolved parents or significant others
- Overreaction to setbacks
- Lack of fun and enjoyment

To promote player engagement, a coach must do the following.

- Be humble and player-centred—a good listener.
- Be supportive—a belief partner.
- Recognise and reinforce any improvement—be a cheerleader.

- Challenge yet remain warm—be tough but supportive.
- Persuade not order—sell, don't yell.
- Treat all players fairly—be respectful.

The coach is not solely responsible for such engagement. Depending on age, players are also much affected by parental attitudes and the influence of their peer group and significant others in their lives. Coaches should aim to establish a coaching environment that embraces everyone and creates enthusiasm for the learning process. Players who fail to engage are generally those whose ego gets in the way of team involvement (not being able to move from 'me' to 'we') or those who cannot overcome the fear of being embarrassed.

Ten Steps to Engaging in Soccer

1. Being from a soccer family
2. Playing in the backyard
3. Having a dream
4. Having a good first experience
5. Having a caring coach
6. Being rewarded for each success
7. Seeing mistakes as learning
8. Having respect from peers
9. Overcoming performance fears
10. Learning to persist

Coaches wishing to assess the level of engagement at their club should use table 1.1 as a guideline.

Inspiration

At the start of the season the team at Middlesbrough FC had agreed to a vision for the season, which included winning a cup competition. They had committed to this goal, dealt with plenty of adversity on the way but now were in the final and about to leave the hotel to travel to the stadium. The players were ushered into a side room. They sat in silence as the lights dimmed and the screen lit up with a film of all their great moments and goals on their cup journey. Accompanying the pictures was the voice of Al Pacino with the words of his famous pregame 'Inches' speech from the movie *Any Given Sunday*. When the film finished the players filed out, boarded the bus, scored two goals in the first seven minutes and won the cup final. This truly inspirational coaching moment gave the team a winning edge.

TABLE 1.1   Check the Level of Engagement at Your Club

	We do this well	We need to do better
Our players feel secure and are looked after.		
Our team are a community with togetherness.		
We share winning and losing together.		
We deal with setbacks well.		
The atmosphere is usually calm and informal.		
Players enjoy coming to practice.		
Everything is planned and prepared.		
There is purpose in everything we do.		
Our players are offered the best teaching.		
We treat mistakes as part of learning.		
Coaches listen as well as speak.		
Players' feelings are important to us.		
We balance praise and criticism well.		
We know when to work and when to rest.		
We praise in public and criticise in private.		
We focus on excellence, not just results.		
Communication is everything to us.		
Our players accept their responsibilities.		
Our players understand their jobs on the field.		
Our players understand others' roles.		
Everyone is clear on our targets.		
Practice is varied, challenging and fun.		
The head coach is inspirational.		
Our players can get all the help they want.		
Bad news is dealt with honestly, face to face.		
Achievements are celebrated and rewarded.		

Inspiring Young Players

I use the following passage to encourage young players (especially female players) to stand out for their team, to be willing to let their light shine.

Who Am I to Be Brilliant?

Our worst fear is not that we are inadequate; our deepest fear is that we are powerful beyond measure. It is our light, not our darkness that frightens us. We ask ourselves, 'Who am I to be brilliant, gorgeous, talented and fabulous?' Actually, who are you not to be? You are a child of God; your playing small doesn't serve the world. There is nothing enlightened about shrinking so that other people won't feel insecure around you. We were born to make manifest the glory of God within us. It is not just in some of us, it is in everyone; and as we let our own light shine we unconsciously give others the permission to do the same. As we are liberated from our own fear, our presence automatically liberates others.

Marianne Williamson quoted by Nelson Mandela

The pursuit of excellence is demanding and almost always involves setbacks as well as gains, anxiety as well as confidence. At such key moments for a team, the power of inspiration is a powerful card for the coach to play.

Inspiration can come from a number of directions—the coach, a player, a visiting speaker, a book, a poem, a film clip and so on. The key is timing. The coach realises that the team are anxious and beginning to disconnect from the purpose and is able to produce an inspirational moment to give them renewed enthusiasm and energy.

The power of inspiration to engage players is that positive ideas release positive emotions, which in turn generate high and positive energy. Champions usually have the ability to release this strong emotional power when needed.

Coach Stuart Lancaster was tasked with reinspiring and reengaging a failed England rugby team. He came up with the idea of inspiring the players by reminding them why they chose to play and how their participation had influenced the significant people in their lives. With wonderful timing just as preseason training started to bite, the coach presented each player with a folder containing one page from his parents explaining how proud they were of their son for making the team; one page each from the three other most significant people who had influenced the player's career, again expressing their pride; and a final page restating the team purpose and the contribution each player could make.

The effect was dramatic. The team were inspired and emotionally connected to their unifying purpose. This translated into performance, and the team met every one of their agreed targets.

Vision Into Action

A Japanese proverb says: 'Vision without action is a dream. Action without vision is a nightmare'.

An agreed team purpose and players who are willing to engage in the process of achieving is a great start. Next, the coach has to turn intention into action. Based on experience and philosophy, coaches must decide for their particular team and level of competition the right way to turn mental commitment into physical delivery.

One successful women's soccer coach takes the shared vision and purpose of her team and has it made into a poster. She has several copies made, and in an early-season ceremony she asks all the players to read and then sign the poster. Copies are then displayed in the team rooms. During the season the coach occasionally reminds them what they committed to.

Rosabeth Moss Kanter in her wonderful book *Confidence* (2004) describes four key enabling conditions for team success:

1. A real team with compelling direction
2. An enabling structure of meaningful tasks and clear standards
3. Expert coaching
4. A supportive environment where effort is rewarded

Coaches should consider this 10-stage plan to turn vision into action and optimize performance excellence:

Stage 1. Establish an inspirational vision—where do the team want to go?

Stage 2. Ensure that everybody is committed—get everybody to buy in.

Stage 3. Connect the dream with the journey ahead—establish the training regime and set goals.

Stage 4. Get engagement to the hard work of preparation.

Stage 5. Overcome the competitive hurdles—feed off the strength of team purpose.

Stage 6. Stay connected to the vision—measure progress constantly.

Stage 7. Hold your nerve—have the discipline to stay with the vision.

Stage 8. Reward productivity and success.

Stage 9. Reinforce the commitment to the dream—we are on our way.

Stage 10. Deliver consistently—win repeatedly.

Importance of Passion

It's crucial, it's vital, this desire, dedication, commitment. Passion can move mountains, in everything, in any job. It's crucial, but if you are going to have passion as a footballer you need to have it all week, not just on a Saturday. In training sessions . . . it's important to show those habits of passion, dedication and desire. The desire to suffer. Only if you are capable of suffering can you have satisfaction—otherwise it is difficult. You have to work.

Paolo Di Canio, manager, Sunderland FC (Edwards 2013)

Such a plan to deliver a team vision into action takes consistent effort and discipline. Coaches have to keep their team aligned to their purpose every day by asking such questions as What are you trying to accomplish? and What have you done today to bring you closer to your goals?

Many teams start the season full of intention, but some do not have the mental toughness to match their passion. When basketball coach Phil Jackson (2013) reflected on the NBA championships he won with the Chicago Bulls, he stressed the team's strength of purpose: 'We had absolutely everything in place that we needed to fulfil our destiny—talent, leadership, attitude, and unity of purpose.'

All coaches are seeking the kind of player behaviour that generates consistent achievement. The strongest foundation for such behaviour comes from establishing a clear, shared vision, supported by agreed on and well-maintained culture and values. When combined with positive relationships that create a high level of player engagement, the right preconditions are put in place to develop a collective mindset that can ensure a committed and rewarding team performance.

A COACH'S STRATEGY TO UNITE THE TEAM

Frank, an outstanding academy U18 coach, is team orientated and spends a lot of time finding a purpose that will glue his team together. He is aware that players have personal agendas in the locker-room. Some players are seeking a professional contract at the end of the season, whereas others just want to continue to improve and see what happens. Frank and his assistant Paul have lots of experience, so they talk to the players about the U18 teams of the past and why certain teams succeeded while others failed and which players went on to be successful and why. The lesson emphasised is that success is gained only by a cohesive team who commit to the hard work of being excellent. Players prosper only in a team who are bound together by a common vision and purpose. The coaches spell out the non-negotiables of becoming top players in a top team. Frank treats his players fairly, but not equally. He knows that he must prioritise limited coaching time and focus more on the players who produce most on game day, the ones seeking a future in the game. He uses Paul, a former outstanding professional, as a source of inspiration for the team, often asking Paul to reinforce coaching points with vivid illustrations. These coaches get a great response from their teams because they are personable and consistently apply a tough-love approach. They challenge and support all their players, although they do have a policy of being tougher on the most talented. Playing for these coaches is not easy, but their sense of purpose and enthusiasm seems to infect the players. Every so often Frank reflects on progress. Why are we here? Where are we now? Where do we want to go? What do we need to do better? Coaches get the players they deserve, and Frank and Paul's ability to establish a clear unifying purpose and a focus on progress produces a disciplined, high-value team from which many go on to further success.

Chapter 2

CREATING POSITIVITY

Coach Tom Bates took an optimistic Birmingham U15 team and parents to compete in the annual Liverpool Tournament. The team won their opening game, but in the next game they lost heavily to Liverpool. Both team and parents changed their view of the situation; optimism was replaced by fear, and energy was replaced by passivity. Tom, a coach and performance psychologist, called a meeting of the team and parents. He told them they would win the tournament and challenged anybody to answer the question, 'Why not?' Again and again Tom asked, 'Why not?' until the group changed their definition of the situation. Birmingham beat Liverpool 3-0 in the final.

A team with a winning mindset are characterised by confidence, focus, conversation, smiles, eye contact and hustle and bustle. This team believe that what they have in their mental locker is enough to win. A team with a losing mindset behave with anxiety, passivity, silence, lack of engagement and eye contact and a general withdrawal from the situation. This team hope they will win but don't really believe it.

Meeting the challenge of soccer requires both physical talent and mental strength. Such mental strength in action is defined and explained in terms of the mindset of each player and the collective mindset of the team (see figure 2.1). Winning begins internally by creating a determined and focused mindset and then operates externally by driving talent potential. Talent without a strong, positive mindset is invariably wasted.

FIGURE 2.1 Results begin with positive thinking.

Teams undoubtedly perform better when they are in a positive mind-set. Their general optimism and belief trigger good feelings, overcome performance anxiety and provide a powerful energy. Teams with a pessimistic mindset often get in their own way, and talent is overwhelmed by general negativity and low energy. The positive team play with their foot on the gas, whereas the negative team have their foot on the brake. In season 2013–14 Derby County FC scored more goals than any other team in the English Championship League simply because the new coach, Steve McClaren, allowed and encouraged the team to take their foot off the brake. Incidentally, Steve shows his complete trust in his team by being one of the few professional coaches who watch the game from high up in the stands.

A positive mindset is a weapon to win as well as a condition that is healthier, more enjoyable and more productive. To achieve this, coaches must overcome the many threats to mindset that can occur before, during or after games. The coach who builds and maintains a positive mindset has a team with the mental strength to cope with the many negatives whilst being encouraged and energised by the positives in any situation. This idea is reinforced by Gene Harker in his book *Leadership Intelligence* (2014, p 141):

> Whereas negativity narrows our perspective, positivity elicits a very different response, motivating us to broaden our understanding and build on our experience. It opens our intellect to new possibilities leading to better problem solving and enhanced creativity. We naturally turn to that which is positive, opening our minds to take in as much as we are able. It inspires us to actively seek opportunities and to interact more richly with our environment. Positive emotions help us to adapt to and recover more quickly from negative experiences. They make a significant contribution to our intellectual, physical, social, and psychological resources.

Deciding to Be Positive

Top teams have mental and emotional skills that separate them from the pack. The defining skill of the great teams is their ability to stay positive under pressure. All teams face a constant stream of challenging situations, but great teams respond better. As part of the daily process of building the talent base, they also develop mental toughness—a frame of reference that sees all challenges as positive opportunities to excel.

Teams pay a price to gain such mental toughness. By persisting through the bad times, a team eventually build such a sense of self-belief that they believe they can steer any situation in their favour, always wanting

---

Theatre of Dreams

When working with Manchester United in their era of dominance, I made an observation in the tunnel as both teams emerged from their locker-rooms to walk onto the field at the aptly named Theatre of Dreams. The sheer size, history, tradition and image of the stadium, not to say the 75,000 fans waiting, at times definitely cast the team in red as fighters and the visitors as potential victims. The two differing definitions of the situation clearly influence the subsequent performance. In season 2010–2011 United won every game at home bar one, which they drew on an off day!

---

to be in the game and have the last shot. Such an ability to frame each challenge in a positive way is the hallmark of a champion.

How teams define a challenging situation in soccer shapes and drives performance. All performance starts in the mind as players individually and collectively seek answers to these questions:

- What exactly is the challenge we face today?
- What do we know of our opponents?
- What is our record against them?
- How strong are we as a team?
- Who will lead us into battle?
- Are we confident?
- How much do we want this?
- What are the risks?
- What are the expectations of others?
- What are the consequences of failure?

The answers to these questions define the situation as perceived by the players, their level of confidence and subsequent game behaviour.

A fundamental difference between winners and losers, fighters or victims, is that the winners and fighters learn to define every competitive situation as a challenge and not as a threat. The following Theatre of Dreams story shows that in the Ferguson era, the Manchester United manager and his team were completely unafraid of the opposition and the occasion. They performed with a mentally tough mindset based on total positivity.

The Growth Mindset

Mindset development—learning to be positive and mentally strong—begins the day a young boy or girl starts playing soccer. The link between mind and body ensures that although coaches might be focusing on physical, technical and tactical skills, they are inevitably teaching mental and emotional skills in parallel.

Carol Dweck (2006) distinguishes between a growth mindset and a fixed mindset.

Fixed	Growth
• Talent, not effort • Outcome, not process • Establish superiority • React to setbacks • Avoid risk	• Work in progress • Focus on process • Love the challenge • Deal with setbacks • Continual improvement

When a team are dominated by a fixed mindset, they focus on the result, value talent and not effort, avoid risk and deal with setbacks badly. A team characterised by a growth mindset embrace challenges, concentrate on the process, see achievement as work in progress, deal with setbacks as a learning experience and value the hard work of preparation.

Dweck established the three rules that characterise fixed and growth behaviours.

Fixed	Growth
1. Look talented at all costs. 2. Don't work too hard or practise too much. 3. When faced with setbacks run away, conceal deficiencies.	1. Learn, learn, learn. 2. Work with passion and dedication—effort is the key. 3. Embrace mistakes and confront deficiencies.

Early influences to develop and nurture a growth mindset are vital. The work of youth coaches in a club or academy should focus on developing the right attitude as much as developing physical and technical skills. Dweck emphasises the importance of a growth mindset for soccer players:

> Recently we conducted a study of college soccer players. We found that the more a player believed athletic ability was a result of effort and practice rather than just natural ability, the better the player performed over the next season. What they believed about their coach's values was even more important. The athletes who believe their coaches prized effort and practice over natural ability were even more likely to have a superior season.

Positive coaching should begin with young players to develop a growth mindset.

Starting at the earliest opportunity, coaches should be shaping positivity and growth mindsets in their young players by encouraging learning, passion, dedication, responsibility and resilience. Coaching a team to develop a growth mindset involves the following principles:

- Don't judge—teach!
- Challenge players to learn and grow.
- Present all skills as learnable with effort and practice.
- Avoid describing players as talented (stop worshipping!).
- Value effort—praise learning and passion.
- Be tough on the 'talented'—demand more.
- Provide constant feedback to support learning—do not protect ego.
- Encourage self-management—players taking responsibility.
- See mistakes as learning opportunities.

- Be optimistic and patient—it's a work in progress.
- Ask great questions—then stand back and listen.
- Measure progress where possible and reward.
- Use setbacks to teach resilience and perseverance.
- Focus on the process and let the score take care of itself.

Competitive Challenge

Figure 2.2 sets out the three main ways soccer teams can interpret the competitive challenge facing them. The key to a good performance is defining the situation positively and seeing the game as winnable. Teams with less talent have won big games because they had defined the game as winnable and played confidently without fear. Table 2.1 shows the differences in attitude—and therefore emotion, energy and performance—when players choose a positive mindset.

Coaches build winning teams by teaching players to perceive the challenge of soccer positively. Coaches must remove any fear and constantly emphasise the need to deal with situations rather than react to them. The first is a thoughtful process recalling past training in similar situations, and the latter is an emotional knee-jerk response.

The late, great English coach Dave Sexton once told me, 'Coaches paint pictures, the simpler the better'.

Coach Sexton saw football as a game of unfolding pictures (situations). The art of practice was to prepare players by presenting similar pictures and teaching players to deal with them. He saw practice as rehearsal. Game day should offer no surprises.

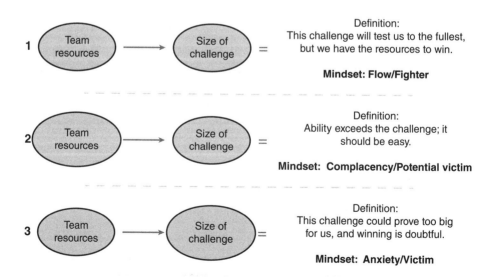

FIGURE 2.2   The mindset of the team after comparing their perceived resources (ability to win) against the perceived size of the challenge (danger of losing).

TABLE 2.1 Characteristics of Positive and Negative Mindsets

Positive mindset	Negative mindset
I am in control.	I am anxious and a little sick.
I am enthusiastic.	I don't feel ready.
I will be at my best today.	I worry about my weaknesses.
I focus on what I can control.	I (we) will struggle today.
I am confident; I know my job.	My (our) opponent look good, big, and tough.
I always recover from setbacks.	People expect too much of me
I am more determined than my opponent is.	I have no confidence in my coach and teammates.
I am full of energy.	I feel tired.
I will persist.	I'm finding it hard to focus.
I can handle any consequences.	I worry about losing face.

Mindset Challenge

The mindset challenge for all soccer players when faced with demanding situations is to take responsibility and deal with them. If successful, players can store their response for future use. If unsuccessful, they and their coach have a learning opportunity.

The what-if exercise in figure 2.3 illustrates a way that coaches can help prepare their teams to take responsibility in a game by rehearsing possible scenarios beforehand.

Figure 2.3   What-If Exercise

In this meeting-room exercise, the team learns the difference between defining a situation positively or negatively.

1. The coach asks the team a what-if question such as the following: What if you are playing away to the champion team? What if you concede an equalising goal with 10 minutes left?
2. The team define the situation positively and negatively.
3. The team consider what they might say positively and negatively.
4. The team consider how they might feel positively and negatively.
5. The team assess their physical response positively and negatively.
6. The team describe their likely performance on the field positively and negatively.
7. The coach and team compare the differences between their positive and negative definitions of the what-if scenario. The team make a decision—if this happens in the future, we will…

One of the key problems I encounter, especially in youth soccer, is that of overcoaching. Coaches are desperate to win. They try to define every soccer situation for their team. By failing to teach personal and collective responsibility, an opportunity to develop mental toughness is lost. When coaches get out of the way of their young players, they allow room for them to learn how to deal with challenging situations and take responsibility for their own destiny

Developing the Fighter Mindset

Soccer, like life, is a series of situations that must be dealt with, for better or worse. Some situations will be common and familiar, such as a centre-back heading a cross clear, and some will be less usual, such as a team dealing with the unexpected sending off of a key player.

Teams, often led by the dominant players, constantly make judgements on their ability to meet such challenges. If they think they can meet the challenge, they adopt a fighter mindset. If they think they can't meet the challenge, they adopt a victim mindset.

When coaches recognise the distinction between the fighter mindset and the victim mindset, they have a much clearer understanding of both player and team mindset. Key questions can be raised:

- How do we build a fighter mindset?
- Which players are inclined to be fighters?
- Which players are inclined to become victims?
- How do we turn a victim back into a fighter?
- What soccer situations turn the mindset of the team from fighter to victim?
- When do we demonstrate fighter mindset, and when do we model victim mentality?

Victim Mindset

Happy to be mediocre
Comfortable with losing
Accepts defeat too easily
Resists learning new things
Can't accept criticism
'Dies' after a mistake
Full of excuses
Never takes responsibility
Blames others
Hides when pressure is on
Finds small injuries
Blames surroundings
Won't communicate and sulks
Chooses victim friends

What coaches must convey to their players and team is that mindset is always a choice. Teams are only fighters or victims because they have chosen to be one or the other at that moment. The job of coaches is to teach players that although they cannot always choose the situation they find themselves in—bad things happen—they can always choose their responses.

Victims Love Excuses

Steve Round, when assistant manager of Everton FC, was on the team bus travelling to Sunderland for an away Premier League match. Despite police outriders the bus became blocked by heavy traffic. As the players realised they would be late and would have to abandon their normal prematch routines, they went quiet and their enthusiasm and energy died. Steve recognised the onset of victim mentality and strode down the bus telling the team, 'Do not use this as an excuse! Great teams deal with these moments'.

Everton went back into fighter mode and won 2-0.

Changing the Story

An American college soccer coach phoned me recently and bemoaned his present situation. He likened the circumstance to a perfect storm where everything that can go wrong does go wrong.

The coach explained that in two days his team would face the number one ranked team in the nation at home in front of their largest crowd ever and with national television covering the game.

The problems were that the team were having a poor season, many of the senior starters were injured, four key players had just been suspended for breaking team rules, and the team would include several 18-year-old freshmen, at least two of whom would be making their debut.

After listening carefully I told the coach I didn't like the story and asked him to call me back in an hour with a different story. At first confused, the coach reluctantly agreed.

One hour later I received a phone call from a much more upbeat and positive coach. Although realistic about the challenges, he was optimistic about the chance of a positive outcome. He had reviewed the situation and decided that although his opponents might be superior technically and tactically, he saw no reason why they could not be outmatched physically and mentally.

The coach's game plan would therefore be based on attitude, energy and emotion—a high-tempo pressing game for the whole 90 minutes. He also decided that if he was at his coaching best on the night, he could both inspire his team and outcoach his rival.

His text immediately after the game read: 'Won 2-0, boys brilliant, season turned round. Thanks!'

The coach had learned some key lessons:

- If you don't like how you feel, change the story!
- All performance is driven by attitude.
- Never underestimate the power of a positive team mindset to win even the biggest games.

The story illustrates that although team mindset is a powerful weapon, it is effective only when coaches create a positive and optimistic environment around the team. When coaches face the inevitable negative situations that occur during a season, their challenge is to find a way to change the story and thus reframe the mindset. The key effect of optimism is in raising energy levels. A team's most valuable asset is energy, and energy comes from positive thinking—'We can!' When a team change their thinking, they change their self-talk, feelings and energy levels.

Key questions for the coach are the following:

- Who provides positive energy for the team?
- Who takes energy away?
- What are the things that give the team high energy?
- What are the energy killers?
- When do I help, and when do I hinder?

Battling Negativity

As the challenge of soccer increases, the battle to maintain positive energy becomes an everyday fight against a stream of potential negatives. The key is identifying and reframing negatives into challenges, not threats. What defeats adversity is continual positive energy, optimism, purpose, passion, enthusiasm, joy and the desire to achieve. Positivity drives production. Harker (2014, p 145) found in a study that high-performance management teams in industry who expressed support or appreciation six times more frequently than they expressed disapproval, sarcasm or cynicism generated better performance outcomes. Champion teams behave like champions long before they become champions.

Tim Grover (2013, p 8), a physical trainer to some of America's greatest athletes, powerfully describes what happens to a player-leader when negativity takes over:

Player Guidelines to Building a Positive Mindset

Identify all the reasons you play soccer and write them down.

Read them before every practice and game.

See yourself as a good player—think positively.

Remember that you have great strengths as well as some weaknesses.

Set yourself some goals and check your progress.

Always give 100 per cent effort.

You are a work in progress—keep learning.

Be passionate about everything you do.

Take pride in bouncing back from setbacks.

Accept any responsibility offered.

He was so distracted by his fear of losing that he couldn't focus on what he had to do to win, couldn't stem the wave of frustration and emotion that was drowning all his natural ability and confidence.

That's how great teams lose: The leader doesn't show up. He's not confident, he's not cool, he's not on his game, and it comes out in little ways he might think no one else perceives. But you can be sure everyone picks up on it and panics.

The energy sapper is negativity, which is fuelled by fear. A small measure of fear of failure can be a motivating factor, but teams who play with excessive fear are always vulnerable to changing circumstances. When they go down a goal early in the game, such teams define the circumstance negatively: 'We have lost now!' The resultant negative self-talk and emotion causes a decline in energy, and they give up on the game.

Unfortunately, the prevailing emotion in many teams is fear of

- a strong opponent,
- failure or embarrassment,
- making mistakes,
- the coaches,
- other people's opinions,
- not meeting expectations or
- the consequences of defeat.

With the increasing pressure to achieve comes an increase in fear of failure. Coaches and players must be stronger than any one result and build the mental and emotional muscle needed to cope with situations that might be seen as threatening.

Hopes and Fears Team Exercise

Coaches can use this start-of-season exercise to create a common and positive team mindset.

All team players have to identify on separate cards one key hope for the team and one key fear. Players do not write their names on the cards. The coach collects all the cards in a hat and then redistributes them so that each person has someone else's hope and fear cards. The players then in turn read out their hope cards, and the coach makes a list on the board.

The players then read out their fear cards. The coach discusses with the players the nature of each fear recorded and ways that it can be overcome.

With fear out of the way, the coach returns to the hope list and ends the meeting on a positive note. The hope list is then placed in a prominent position and referred to as the season progresses.

The Lewis review (2007) on English soccer academies recommended a switch of focus from results to development:

> Coaches are therefore advised to monitor regularly the fears of failure of adolescent football players and pay close attention to their coping responses to failure and their fear of failure. They can help players develop and employ adaptive coping skills (i.e., that allow for positive psychological adjustment) to manage these stressors.

The first step to coping with any fear present is always to believe that great things are possible and to create optimism. Realistic optimism is a powerful force in coping with fear. Coaches need to check how their teams match up to the optimism of the great teams who do the following:

- Choose to be successful
- See opportunities, not threats
- Embrace the discomfort of aiming high
- Take more risks and achieve greater returns
- Given the choice, back themselves
- Believe in control, not luck
- Believe that good fortune is earned
- Believe the force of their personality can steer things in their favour
- Always want the last shot of the game

Achieving a Positive Mindset

Here are some common factors that apply when teams build and maintain a positive mindset.

Performance Follows Mindset

Great deeds follow intention, desire and perseverance. These three attributes fuel the physical, technical and tactical responses that the coach is seeking from his or her players.

- Intention gives players direction and purpose.
- Desire builds the passion that creates the necessary energy.
- Perseverance ensures commitment and the overcoming of obstacles.

Coaches know that they cannot achieve success with players or teams that lack these qualities. However coaches know that they will get a positive performance from players or teams that have these qualities.

With a strong positive mindset even the slightly less talented team can aim to win because their intention, desire and perseverance can make a winning difference.

Dreams and Goals Fuel Mindset

As described in chapter 1, a positive mindset is triggered and maintained by an intense passion to achieve a dream or a goal (the reason why) that has been set. Great coaches know that they must constantly reinforce the team's purpose so that their players make extraordinary efforts. The harder the challenge is, the more coaches must regularly reconnect their players to their dreams and goals. This burst of inspiration shapes positive thinking and emotions and releases the energy needed to continue to pursue the team vision.

Mindset Determines Altitude

Mindset is the determining factor that differentiates between teams of equal talent; winners think like winners. Bill Russell, the former Boston Celtics basketball great, in his timeless book *Second Wind* (1980), sums this up beautifully:

> Even with all the talent, the mental sharpness, the fun, the confidence and your focus honed down to winning, there'll be a level of competition where all that evens out. Then the pressure builds and for a champion it's a test of heart. . . . Heart in champions has to do with the depth of your motivation and how well your mind and body react to pressure. It's concentration —that is, being able to do what you do under maximum stress.

Mindset Is a Choice

A team's state of mind in any given situation is their choice; optimistic or pessimistic, confident or anxious, strong or weak (see figure 2.4). Coaches have to learn to employ a diversity of strategies to influence a team's thinking, depending on the specific context. A range of such strategies are developed and illustrated as you make your way through parts II and III of this book. In the end, the power of the team is released only if they choose a positive competitive mindset based on confidence and toughness. In soccer it's not always the best team who win but the best team on the day; the team with less talent can win because they choose a tougher competitive mindset than the team with more talent.

Mindset Is Personal Responsibility

If performance is driven by mindset and mindset is a choice, then players and teams must take full responsibility for any mindset weakness that leads to poor performance. Coaches must stress that their teams need to become and stay strong minded to win consistently. Such mental preparation is as important as physical, technical and tactical preparation. When

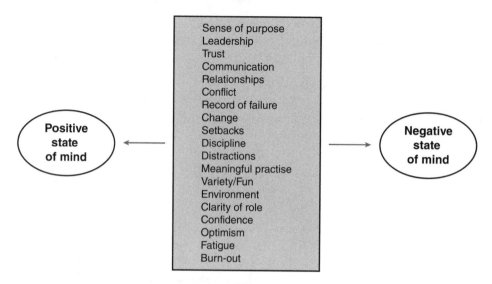

FIGURE 2.4 Mindset is a choice—potential influences on a team's state of mind to become positive or negative.

coaches identify poor performance as a failure of weak thinking, anxiety, loss of focus, loss of emotional control and so on, they must not allow blaming but instead teach players and teams to accept responsibility.

Mindset Grows When Nurtured

If a coach wants to build a positive and resilient team state of mind, she or he must target and nurture effort and consistent improvement. John Wooden, the late, great basketball coach, was a perfect example:

> What did he give them? He gave them constant training in the basic skills, he gave them conditioning, and he gave them mindset. When players coasted during practice, he finished it—they had lost the opportunity to become better that day! He challenged, taught and nurtured. Of course, the real competition he was preparing for was life—he taught them the values and characteristics that could make them not only good players but also good people (Thompson 2003).

Experience Builds Mindset

Like physical, technical and tactical skills, mindset needs to be practised. It can be built with experience. The first time a team go to Old Trafford, the home of Manchester United, the experience is daunting. The team's definition of the situation might easily lead to a state of mind that anticipates defeat. But after a team have experienced the visit four or five times, they can deal with the distraction and focus on the soccer. With experience, they are more likely to have a positive competitive mindset.

In this way coaches often 'buy' experience for new and younger players because they realise that only by getting time in the competitive arena can young players build the mental strength of a winner and contribute fully to the team. In the 2014 World Cup in Brazil the England manager, Roy Hodgson, made a brave and far-sighted decision. Realising that the team were unlikely to reach the final stages, Coach Hodgson boldly selected a squad that included a significant number of young and inexperienced players. The team failed in terms of results, but they gained enormously in terms of experience. The benefits of this will be seen in major tournaments over the next 10 years.

Mindset Is Strengthened by Recovery From Failure

The journey to excellence is not a straight line for teams, and the prospect of failure is ever present. Such setbacks are the greatest threat to the positive thinking of a team, so the coach must deal with the situation in a way that does not damage the team. Martin Seligman (1998), the great advocate of positive psychology, stresses that the difference between winners and losers is how they interpret such setbacks: 'Individuals and teams who possess a more optimistic explanatory style have more positive outcomes, especially after experiencing a setback or defeat'.

If coaches interpret setbacks as personal ('We are hopeless'), permanent ('This always happens') and universal ('We never win away from home'), then the team are drifting into a state that Seligman calls learned helplessness.

But if the setback is interpreted as impersonal ('Things went against us today'), temporary ('Just a bad day at the office') and specific ('Losing today does not make us a bad team'), then a positive mindset is not damaged and can even be strengthened from the experience. When a coach takes over a losing team, he or she can often quickly assess the team's mindset as learned helplessness. The previous coach failed to interpret setbacks in a way that maintained positive hope. The new coach can rebuild mindset by repeatedly saying the following:

- 'You are good players going through a bad time'.
- 'Even in that defeat I could see lots of things improving'.
- 'If we keep working and believing, things will change'.

Coaches affect the way their team think and feel by seeing the positive things that they can do and not dwelling on what they can't.

KEY TEAM MEETINGS SET A POSITIVE ENVIRONMENT

Chris, an enthusiastic and thoughtful U18 boys coach, is committed to building a coaching environment that creates and nurtures positivity. He knows from his own playing career that no one wants to play for a pessimistic coach. He also knows that U18 players are at a critical career point where their entry into senior soccer, college or professional, is being assessed. The mindset of the players needs to remain optimistic, enthusiastic and energetic during a long, challenging season.

Coaches' meeting. Chris calls a meeting of his support staff and outlines his plan for creating a positive environment.

- Everyone must model positivity in every practice and game.
- Players will be challenged but always supported.
- Players will be taught to look for the positives in every situation.
- Feedback will be realistic but end with an action plan for improvement.
- Setbacks must not be allowed to damage self-belief.
- Fun, purpose and challenge must overcome anxiety and fear.
- Coaches must teach but avoid overcoaching and causing confusion.
- Players must work hard but not be overtrained.
- All must hold their nerve regardless of results.

Coach Chris believes in shared ownership at the U18 level. He always gives the players the feeling that it is their team and that he and his staff are there to help.

Players' meeting. Chris meets the players for 15 minutes and emphasises these points:

- The reason you are in this room is that you are a good player—never forget that!
- This club have a proud history, and you should feel honoured.
- Your responsibility is to do your best by challenging yourself every day.
- Focus on developing your game, not the results.
- The only important expectations are yours, the team's and the coaches'.
- Don't waste time on what you can't control.
- Ask yourself what you can do to be a good team member.
- Mistakes will happen—deal with them.
- Make good lifestyle choices—you cannot be a part-time athlete.
- Remember that you can win only if the team win—team first!

In two quick but powerful meetings, Chris established the rules of a positive environment for both the staff and the players. Chris does not call many meetings during the season, but he values these two meetings in establishing the team environment as optimistic, positive and supportive—the basis for success on the field.

Chapter 3

FOCUSING CHALLENGE

When talking with teams about building a strong competitive mindset, I like to refer to a scene from the film *A League of Their Own*. When the female baseball star is asked by the team manager why she is quitting the team, she tells him it just got too hard. He responds, 'It's supposed to be hard. If it wasn't hard, everyone would do it. The hard is what makes it great.'

What sets soccer apart from many of the activities that young people of today participate in is the level of challenge—failing is quite possible! A key lesson in soccer development for young players is learning to do the hard things—to become tough minded.

When soccer teams agree a unifying purpose, they are committing themselves to a hard, challenging journey. The teams that can focus on the challenges, fulfil their purpose and achieve their dreams are usually the mentally toughest. Building that mental toughness is the task of coaches regardless of their team's age, gender or level of competition. Every coach has to adopt a coaching style and plan a programme that converts a team vision to everyday action, eventually building to ultimate fulfilment.

We Do Tough

When I told a struggling U18 girls team the story from *A League of Their Own*, the coach seized on the idea. The next time the girls arrived for practice, they found T-shirts in their locker-room emblazoned with 'WE DO TOUGH'—a message that they now had to live up to!

The key to winning soccer games is being willing to face and overcome the challenge of the opposition. The collective team mindset has to be sharpened every day by an environment of challenge at practice. Coaches have to clarify the challenges both on and off the field for the team, for the tactical units within the team and for each player. No progress occurs without direction. The coach as leader is the model of the team vision and direction and is a powerful influence in the focus of the team's mental strength. Good coaches know how they want the game to be played and what the team in front of them are capable of doing. Then they work backwards to set standards of performance that the team must meet in every practice. Successful teams have a mindset that is open to meeting the challenges that the coach sets before them by being coachable and willing to work hard. After this environment is established, new players joining the team are likely to accept the tough standards already set.

Remember these key statements:

- Attitude is free.
- Desire costs nothing.
- Passion has no price tag.
- You pay nothing for commitment.
- Today's effort becomes tomorrow's result.

Focusing Challenge in Practice

Challenge brings stress, and practice teaches adaptation to stress. The coach rehearses the team for the stress of game day by creating an environment of challenge. The strength of team mindset is fashioned by the focus and intensity that players apply to every practice session.

Practice must always be an opportunity to teach players how to adapt to stress, thrive on challenge and manage the inevitable mistakes and setbacks. Coaches must provide well-planned sessions with direction and purpose that constantly challenge the players. For example, Coach Steve Harrison at Middlesbrough always tested his defensive back four in a session in which they had to defend against a mobile attack of six good academy players. Organisation, shape, discipline, communication and focus were all examined in a tough 45-minute session in which goals conceded led to extra sprints for the defenders at the end of practice. This sort of practice breeds the communal confidence that kicks in on game day.

Colvin (2008, p 7–9) singles out deliberate practice as the factor that shapes great performance: 'Deliberate practice is hard. It hurts. But it works. More of it equals better performance. Tons of it equals great performance'.

> The smarter the preparation is, the tougher the work is.
>
> The greater the confidence is, the smaller the challenge seems.

And Colvin recognises the importance of a mindset that can focus on the challenge: 'The chief constraint is mental, regardless of the field—even in sports, where we might think the physical demands are the hardest. Across realms, the required concentration is so intense that it's exhausting.'

Challenge the Best

When asked to speak to an international team at the start of a new campaign with the goal of winning a World Cup, I offered the following:

I congratulated them on making the room. . . . Many didn't.

I challenged them to win the shirt. . . . Only the best do.

I challenged them to keep their place in the team. . . . Few do.

I challenged them to win something significant. . . . Even fewer do.

I challenged them to become a legend. . . . Reserved for the greats.

Challenge is at the heart of achievement.

He concludes, 'Contemporary athletes are superior not because they're somehow different but because they train themselves more effectively'. A useful checklist for challenging players at practice includes these points:

- Are the players physically prepared?
- Does each player know her or his job on the field?
- Does each player understand the role of her or his unit (e.g., back four defending)?
- Does each player understand the team game plan?
- Does each player know her or his job at set pieces?
- Is each player able to perform these tasks under pressure and fatigue?
- Are the players confident in their ability?

So whilst a team are preparing physically, technically and tactically for an upcoming game challenge, they are also preparing mentally and emotionally. A state of mind that drives and maximises physical talent is not a given, but an accumulation of the strength of thoughts and feelings that come with positive and challenging preparation. How we practise defines who we are; preparation changes expectations.

Preparation, and equally the lack of it, is a significant influence on the team mindset as players cross the white line to face the challenge of opponents. Teams should never be outplayed by either lack of preparation or lack of effort.

Preparing Teams for Challenge

An important element in a coach's development is building an understanding of how to shape a collective team mindset that can face and overcome challenge. Drawing on my work in mentoring coaches, I believe that eight interactive aspects are involved.

1. Process

Building a powerful team mindset takes time and must always be viewed as an ongoing process constantly threatened by change and setbacks. Some coaches deliberately plan a tough preseason schedule to build team toughness. Many great teams have gone through the fire of defeats, setbacks and criticism to emerge with a much stronger competitive state of mind.

Practice has to prepare teams for tough situations. Coaches must create a working environment that can, when needed, simulate game urgency and intensity. This job is much easier when chasing the top spot in a league rather than holding the number one place and being chased. Coaches of teams at the top of a league must fight complacency by insisting on having the same perspective as a chasing team—seeing their teams as perpetual underdogs, always as number two striving to be number one. All opponents should be considered slightly better but beatable with effort. Only hard and challenging work can ensure victory. The attention to the process of achieving excellence leads to the desired outcome.

All coaches want to win, so they can easily become fixated with the outcome, not the process. However, an essential part of my mentoring programme is to help coaches understand that only by having their team focus on the process—playing excellently on defence and offense—can they increase the chances of a successful outcome. The best coaches understand that game-day glory is the direct result of the effort and quality produced throughout practice days and that game-day disappointments point to failings in practice. Taking this step is essential in the maturing of a coach.

2. Competition Is Good

Sport is based on competition. Every time a team play, they face opponents determined to win. Coaches prepare their players' competitive mindset by simulating the challenge, rehearsing in practice what players will face in games. Practice must be challenging and competitive. It must motivate and energise players to give greater effort, strengthen their mental resolve to win and sort out the weak from the strong. It can also help build the confidence and self-belief of winners, evaluate the progress of players and teach self-discipline—passion with control.

> I observed that if individuals who prevail in a highly competitive environment have one thing in common besides success, it is failure—and their ability to overcome it. 'Crash and burn' is part of it, so are 'recovery and reward'. When you do that, the score will take care of itself.
>
> Bill Walsh (2009)

Meeting the challenge in competition comes from challenging and competitive practice.

Good practice for players is working hard, learning and having fun. To prepare for games, however, practice must be a constant challenge of competitive drills and game situations that force players to commit at higher and higher levels. No player or team achieve mental toughness by staying in their comfort zone.

One of the great dangers of achieving success as a soccer team (think about the Brazil 2014 World Cup team) is the tendency to relax and take a foot off the gas. When working with a top team recently, I could clearly see, as an independent observer, that both coaches and players had relaxed their standards. An environment that needs to be constantly challenging had become too comfortable. The team were heading for a fall. To their credit, the coaches immediately recognised the validity of my concerns and reintroduced a higher level of challenge into practice and re-established a more 'uncomfortable' environment. Keeping aware of and countering signs of complacency can be achieved by continual evaluation and appraisal. End-of-practice and weekly reviews introduce regular checks on training and game mindset. Film analysis provides the evidence for answers to tough questions such as these:

- Are we too comfortable?
- Are we working hard enough?
- Are we making progress?
- Who is (and who is not) performing well and why?

Success in soccer is based on talent, passion and a tough, competitive mindset. Such mental strength is built by overcoming the stress of regular competition in practice. From the age of eight onwards, sport offers young players the choice between fight or flight. A healthy combination of challenge and support, appropriate to age, gender and level, ensures an increasingly tough attitude. To build a competitive team mindset, coaches must

- build a competitive element into practice,
- encourage and reward winners,
- teach recovery from losing,
- reinforce constantly what wins,
- increase awareness of what loses
- arouse passion but demand control,
- seize mistakes as teachable moments,
- monitor development as well as results,
- teach the management of conflict and
- learn how to win with style and lose with grace.

World's Greatest Last-Place Finisher

The last event of the 1968 Olympics in Mexico City was the men's marathon. The winner had been finished for two hours when the last-place runner hobbled into the stadium. He limped around the track, crossed the finish line, fell to his hands and knees and kissed the ground. The media surrounded him and learned that he was John Stephen Akhwari from Tanzania. When asked why he kept running, John replied, 'My country sent me 10,000 miles to compete. They didn't send me to start the race; they sent me 10,000 miles to finish the race'.

---

3. Commitment

Commitment is a choice that players make to be loyal to the process of achieving the agreed vision of the team despite the difficulties. Commitment means finishing what you started, following through on what you say you are going to do, valuing your words and keeping your promises. The commitment to work constantly toward an agreed goal binds a team together and creates a strong mindset. Committed teams don't give in easily.

Coaches must insist on appropriate commitment from the U8s to the most experienced professionals. Teams must be taught that hard work, effort and preparation lead to feelings of success and goal achievement, that setbacks will be followed by renewed commitment and that effort and success are constantly linked. Every player must understand the level of commitment required. Coaches need to teach their players to think and behave like champions before they actually become champions.

The Committed Player . . .

1. Always works hard
2. Can produce a little extra
3. Makes things happen
4. Stays in the game, regardless of the score
5. Sees criticism as helpful feedback
6. Is not afraid to fail
7. Recovers well after a mistake
8. Is a team player
9. Never misses practice
10. Makes the right choices, every day

4. Character

Meeting the challenge of competition requires talent but draws heavily on the character of the players and the team. Jamie Carragher, the renowned former Liverpool and England defender, was not the most talented member of the team, but he played over 600 games in the Premier League because of the strength of his character.

Playing soccer is a test of character that forces players to choose responses to a constant stream of challenging situations. Doing the right thing takes considerable willpower. Character is tested when things are not always fair or when mistakes and setbacks happen.

Top players have both talent and character, so in insisting that young players show good values and attitude, the coach is preparing them for the demands of high-level sport. Young players need to learn the following attitude characteristics of top performers:

- Self-belief
- Self-discipline
- Competitive fire (passion)
- Emotional control

- Coachability
- Ability to focus and persist (toughness and resilience)
- Willingness to be part of a team
- Ability to make good life choices

Only under pressure do players demonstrate true character, and for this reason practice must include competition and challenge. Helping young players make the right choices and build strong character is the foundation for their development as players and people.

Coaches teach positive character by

- identifying how character drives successful performance,
- emphasising character as well as talent,
- knowing when performance problems are 'won't do' (an issue of character) rather than 'can't do' (an issue of ability),
- defining the character trait needed to be successful in each practice situation,
- highlighting when character breaks down and reinforcing when it drives success,
- providing character models—visiting speakers, film clips and so on—to illustrate the power of character on performance,
- identifying the non-negotiables of their programme—the player character traits that are required for the coach to work successfully—and
- insisting always that the player is responsible for her or his behaviour and performance and refusing to allow excuses and blaming.

5. Work Ethic

The better the player wants to become, the harder he or she has to work. Ultimately, work ethic is what makes champions. Work ethic is about understanding the cost of success and being willing to pay the price. Victory cannot simply be dreamed about; it has to be earned. The will to work must precede the will to win.

The Right Question

A new coach appointed to a Premier League club soon found one young player who was vastly underachieving. The player was terrified when sent for, fearing the worst. The coach sat him down, gave him a bottle of water, leaned back and said, 'Tell me what I can do to help you be a better player'. The player relaxed, a constructive discussion followed, and he left the room remotivated and with an action plan to work on. He went on to become an outstanding player for the club.

FC Twente in Holland has many talented young players. As at all clubs, occasionally a problem occurs with work ethic. Sometimes players use their talent as an excuse not to work, and sometimes the coach, in awe of their talent, lets them get away with it. In the belief that talent must be made to work hard, director of football Cees Lok introduced an extra session one afternoon each week. In a tough and demanding 90-minute skills session, the staff of the club's senior team coached the talented 15- to 18-year-olds. This 'tough on talent' programme has confirmed the essential relationship between talent, work ethic and achievement.

> **Working Excellently— A Player Code**
>
> Always remember why you play soccer.
> Understand that you are in control.
> Set personal targets.
> Be positive at all times.
> Enjoy, don't endure.
> Learn something new every practice.
> Switch on when working.
> Switch off when recovering.
> See practice as game rehearsal.
> Take responsibility and set your own limits.
> Squeeze every drop out of your potential.
> Never let your teammates down.

Young players of today are turned on by positive, enthusiastic and fair coaches who treat everyone with respect and create a challenging, collaborative and fun environment. They are turned off by cynicism, sarcasm, unfairness and lack of caring.

To establish work ethic and standards, coaches should do the following:

- Understand the work that the team need to do at that point.
- Ensure that all work is relevant to the age, gender and level of the players.
- Always explain why the work is needed.
- Communicate high expectations.
- Inspire and instil belief in the players.
- Set goals to give direction and motivation to the work.
- Encourage all players to work to their maximum potential.
- Challenge the talented players the most.
- Create variety and interest in the practice.
- Establish work as a team ethic.
- Reject mediocrity.
- Always reward good work.
- Model the behaviour they expect from their players.

Five Steps to Player Self-Discipline

1. Decide how you want to behave.
2. Understand that it's hard before it's easy.
3. Refuse to make excuses.
4. Refuse to allow exceptions.
5. If you slip, recover quickly.

6. Discipline

Developing a mentally tough team mindset when facing difficult challenges involves disciplined thinking that leads to disciplined action under pressure. The price of achievement is the discipline to do what is required to be successful. Discipline in practice and team games means being in the right place at the right time, knowing what needs to be done, taking responsibility for doing it, doing it to the standards the team expect and doing it when nobody is watching.

Coaches will not get discipline in game situations unless they insist on it in practice—every practice! This process begins when coaches determine their non-negotiables—the essential rules to which the squad conform. When players accept and follow these rules, the collective mindset of the team is strengthened. Without a common and agreed way of working together, players will follow their personal agendas and discipline is likely to break down.

Many successful coaches limit their non-negotiable rules as far as possible and concentrate on building self-managing and self-disciplined players. They offer shared ownership of all the rules and guidelines to team behaviour that can be negotiable. This discipline is not so much imposed but rather delegated to each player's sense of purpose, pride and accountability.

To build a disciplined team mindset, coaches must do the following:

- Determine the non-negotiables of working together
- Make sure that the non-negotiables are communicated and agreed upon
- Link all agreements to player responsibility
- Only agree on rules that can be enforced
- Emphasise that the welfare of the team comes first in all decisions

7. Focus

Focusing on what needs to be done to be successful is an essential element of a tough mindset. Love of the game, a desire to do well and a fear of failure all contribute to intensity of focus. Soccer is a game of speed, variety, intensity and a continual unfolding of problems to be solved. Teams may start with a good attitude, but the game soon brings the intrusion of negative thoughts—what-ifs—that result in a loss of focus and intensity, made worse by the onset of fatigue. Many goals are scored in periods of the game when team and individual focus falters. Danger times are just before halftime and in the final minutes of the game. In these moments concentration wavers under pressure and fatigue, sometimes to costly effect.

Derby County FC played in the 2014 Championship Playoff Final at Wembley for a place in the Premier League and the huge rewards that victory would bring. After dominating the game and clearly being the better team, a couple of defensive errors in the final minute of the game led to Derby conceding the goal and defeat. Ninety-nine per cent focus often leads to 100 per cent failure!

A focused mindset is one that

- knows what to attend to,
- knows what not to attend to,
- will not be distracted,
- stays in focus as long as necessary, and
- is intense, but not tense.

Focus, like all other mindset skills, must be rehearsed in practice. Players need to know what to focus on and what not to focus on. Coaches must create good mental habits by creating realism and pressure in practice and by preparing the players' thinking and imaging in game scenarios.

8. Tough on Talent

Achievement is based on talent and mindset. Both must be challenged by coaches who want their players to succeed at the highest levels. Coaches must not be in awe of talent or ignore mindset development. Talent is only potential, and it needs character to shape it into performance under pressure. When a player is labelled as talented too early, without reference to mindset qualities and the development of character, initial expectations are usually unfulfilled.

When assessing the talent level of their players, coaches must make the following mindset checks:

- Levels of motivation and commitment—passion to play
- Work ethic—willingness to pay the price
- Readiness to learn—coachable
- Character—ability to cope with the demands
- Competitive fire—needing to win all the time

Buzzwords as Triggers

Coaches can help create focus by giving teams words that trigger an immediate response mentally, emotionally and physically. Brian Ashton, a well-respected rugby coach, changed a team mindset that was passive on defence by deleting the word *defence*: 'We attack with the ball and we *attack* without the ball!' Andy Farrell, once voted the best rugby league player in the world and now a member of the England rugby union coaching team, teaches focus in defence by constantly emphasising the word *bounce!* His teams learn to associate *bounce* with having high energy and passion, sending positive messages to teammates ('I am ready') and sending aggressive messages to opponents ('We are ready').

Buzzwords, as just described, can be an effective teaching tool for improving team focus, and they are popular with younger players. Paul McGuiness, coach at Manchester United Academy, once taught his U12 team the buzzword *chain* to build the concept of togetherness and defensive strength. He built this by

- introducing the word *chain* and asking each player to write down the meaning and draw a chain,
- getting players to move together, link arms and form a chain,
- surprising the team by calling 'Chain' at any stage when they were together as a team and
- calling 'Chain' in games when the team needed defensive togetherness and strength.

Simple, effective, powerful and fun!

- Discipline—staying in control at all times
- Ability to focus—can be trusted in the game
- Ability to persist—staying in the game
- Ability to bounce back—can handle disappointments

Unless the player scores well in these criteria, she or he may profile as high on talent but low on attitude—a notorious underachiever!

Coach Steve Round, former assistant manager at English Premier League clubs Manchester United and Everton, has helped integrate a series of talented youth players into senior teams. He has based this work on the theme 'Tough on Talent'. Instead of being in awe of talented youth and backing away from coaching them, Steve has always believed in being tougher on the talented players than on the rest of the team. He loves their talent but understands that without commitment, effort and the ability to learn every day, it might never flourish.

Steve has these rules:

Fast-Tracking Young Talent

1. Identify talent.
2. Build a player support team.
3. Create a player profile of strengths and weaknesses.
4. Encourage player self-management.
5. Build a five-year career plan.
6. Work every day on the physical, technical and tactical.
7. Work every day on building mental toughness.
8. Teach the athlete's lifestyle.
9. Limit the number of games to avoid burnout.
10. Monitor progress and problems.

- Never be in awe of talent.
- Never label a player talented unless you are sure.
- Create an objective (measured) player profile.
- Maximise strengths and address weaknesses.
- Insist on full commitment in every practice.
- Teach responsibility and accountability.
- Establish clear goals and targets.
- Raise the bar slowly but continually.
- Always praise effort, never the talent.
- Insist on humility—they are ordinary people with extraordinary talent.
- Support the star—don't become the star.
- Be wary of the halo complex—get second or third opinions.
- Be wary of overuse and burnout.

A COACH PREPARES HER TEAM TO FACE CHALLENGE

Stacey, the outstanding coach of an U18 girls team, works every day on shaping her team's mindset to face the challenge of soccer. Knowing that her team lack a little competitive fire, Stacey uses the preseason to build a mindset that competition is good and that it's OK to win. Team meetings focus on building motivation, setting small achievable goals and dealing with winning and losing. Stacey works on both co-operation and competition in practice and always reinforces competitive success with praise whilst urging the losers to bounce back.

Stacey understands that to commit to soccer, girls have to connect to the team, so she builds the team mindset around 'Family, Togetherness and Challenge'. She asks the team to be inclusive, take care of everyone and encourage each other to be the best players they can be. The team agree to commit to the following rules:

- Respecting each other
- Talking constructively
- Encouraging each other
- Putting the team first
- Being ready for practice early
- Attending every practice
- Remaining positive no matter what

Stacey follows these up by relating them to playing and winning.

In this room we are a family, everyone is important, and we take care of each other. This is true off the field, but it must also be true on the field. We have decided to play competitive soccer, and so we must compete. But we will compete together whether you are on the field or on the bench. And by the way, it's OK to stand out—as a family we love our stars. So we work together, we learn together, we compete together, and we win or lose together. But winning is preferable, so let's go practise!

In this way Stacey builds a team mindset that gradually reduces anxiety and begins to embrace competition and challenge. As a result, commitment and work ethic increase, which in turn leads to the confidence of being well prepared. When she is sure that the team can cope, Stacey slowly turns up the challenge to see who has the character to stay committed in the face of pressure. Like any good coach, Stacey expects her leaders to set the example, but because she actively recruits for character as well as talent, she is never surprised when a new player shows leadership.

Stacey's team always overachieves by competing hard, taking the hits, bouncing back and always sticking together!

Chapter 4

ENCOURAGING LEADERS

A wise man, long in football management, said recently that the hardest post to fill in the modern game was not goalkeeper, centre-forward, fullback or any position. It was Great Captain. We won't name the sage, lest the skipper of his present team take offence, but his point was well made and is often echoed. Perhaps the character of the sport's captains has changed in the millionaire era, or possibly the captain with character is becoming an endangered species.

This quotation from a *Sunday Times* article by Ian Hawkey (2005) emphasises a difficulty faced not only by the coaches of millionaires but also by the coaches of younger players, some of whom come from a background of indulgence. Player leadership is becoming increasingly hard to find.

Yet leadership is key to the mindset of a successful soccer team. Teams operate in demanding environments where purpose, motivation and cohesion are always under threat. Good teams stand firm at such times and rely on team leaders to keep everybody on track.

Defining Leaders

A winning team mindset is a combination of the passion to achieve and the mental toughness to do so. These attributes are not shared equally among the players who sit in the locker-room before a big game. The collective team state of mind when they finally cross the white line is probably determined by any combination of the coach, an inspirational player or a small core of influential players.

These leaders will be spreading the word: We can win if we work hard enough, play smart enough, put team interest ahead of our own and continuously focus on getting better, so follow us and we will show you the way.

Such a group will demonstrate leadership in getting the team ready. Whilst the mindsets of some individual players are battling between confidence and anxiety, the leaders step up and interpret the situation in a positive, optimistic way—'We can do it!' Anxious players seize on this definition of the situation and take confidence and energy from their leaders. Leadership in the locker-room is about convincing players they can do things they believed that they were not able to do (see figure 4.1).

> Peer pressure is much more powerful than the concept of a boss. Many, many times more powerful. People want to live up to what is expected of them.
>
> Malcolm Gladwell (2000)

Interpreting the 2014 World Cup game in which Germany beat Brazil 7-1 in those terms would show that it was a clash between character and personality. Brazil had personality but no leadership, whereas Germany had character and leadership all over the field. A system that focused on skill had been beaten by a system that stressed both skill and character. Leadership through personality can break down under pressure or adversity, whereas leadership through character is able to hold firm.

Good coaches understand that a real source of power to drive winning teams comes from the locker-room, where the players decide to commit to the hard work of preparation. They also understand that the locker-room will be dominated by a small core of leaders, often seniors, who define how the team will respond to situations. Malcolm Gladwell's book *The Tipping Point* (2000) offers many examples of the ability of a small group of determined people to shape the thinking and behaviour of

Figure 4.1   Leadership Defined

An exercise with a U15 girls team.

L	Love
E	Effort
A	Action
D	Determination
E	Energy
R	Resilience
S	Style
H	Heart
I	Inspiration
P	Presence

Core Leadership

The most powerful core of players I have ever seen lead was the group of players who had been promoted from the youth team at Manchester United, known as the Class of '92. The Neville brothers, Beckham, Giggs, Scholes and Butt simply overpowered the senior locker-room with their passion to succeed. The captain, Roy Keane, was happy to stand aside to allow the 'kids' to exert massive peer pressure in the locker-room and on the practice field, raising the standard, releasing the emotional power of the team and driving them to the most successful period in the club history.

---

a much larger group. Harnessing the power of peer pressure and getting such a core group onside is essential to the coach who wants to build a winning team mindset.

The decision to be champions comes from the locker-room when teams:

- find a cause they get excited about
- accept responsibility
- take ownership of the journey
- stop blaming others or circumstances and
- find leaders to drive the team forward.

Leadership Mindset

Leadership is a way of thinking. It begins in the head of each player with a desire to achieve and a willingness to take responsibility. Every member of a playing squad has a purposeful role to play and therefore a responsibility to him- or herself, the team and the coaches (see table 4.1). Players should be taught responsibility, individually and collectively, from the very start of their involvement in soccer. The power of a strong, collective team mindset is based upon the conviction that every single player can be trusted to carry out his or her responsibilities.

TABLE 4.1 **Player Responsibilities**

To yourself	To your team	To your coach
Check your motivation.	Do your job.	Be early.
Prepare for each day.	Be enthusiastic.	Be ready to work.
Set personal goals.	Encourage others.	Be coachable.
Believe in yourself.	Always try hard.	Accept decisions.
Live like an athlete.	Be good in bad times.	Seek to improve.

On one of our regular phone calls during which we discussed the mental and emotional state of the FC Twente team, former head coach Steve McClaren said, 'This team is not as good as I want it to be. But it is going to be as good as the players want it to be!'

Steve understood that leadership emerges from the habit of taking responsibility. Certain players will emerge who are capable not only of taking care of their own individual responsibilities but also of helping the team with their collective responsibility, taking the lead and therefore making a difference.

Player leadership can emerge in differing forms:

- A captain who accepts responsibility for representing the team
- An inspirational leader—a talent who inspires the team
- A core group of players determined to succeed
- An emotional leader—a player who can capture the feelings of the team
- The social connector leader—a 'mother hen' figure
- Pop-up leadership—a player nearest to the situation taking charge

When the layers are peeled back to analyse a great team, many of these elements will appear. As discussed later in this chapter, for younger or less talented teams a good solution lies in establishing a small core of players, a leadership group, who share the coach's ambitions and passion and have the ability to spread the message.

A growing trend in soccer is to focus on player 'entitlements'—rights and respect—but young players must learn that responsibility comes first. Every player must learn to take responsibility for her or his actions, and responsibility means being in the right place at the right time doing the right thing to the standard that the coach requires. Especially important is the discipline to continue to do the right things consistently when nobody is watching.

The philosophy at the excellent FC Twente Academy is that to build character, you have to give responsibility. The former director of football, Cees Lok, as a great player in his time, was aware that the building of character must go alongside the development of talent. When young boys and girls enter the academy, they are quickly made aware of their responsibilities. As they progress through the academy, player responsibility is reinforced at every level. The aim (see figure 4.2) is to build the kind of self-disciplined, self-managing players who can emerge as leaders and deal with the tough environment of the first team locker-room. At all times the players are made aware that they have ownership and control of their behaviour, that becoming a soccer player and being in the team is their choice.

FIGURE 4.2 The journey to leadership.

Steve McClaren always tells his players, 'I don't drop you from the team, you drop yourself!'

Finding Leaders

One day at Sunderland FC one of the coaches was bemoaning the lack of leaders in his team. I disagreed and persuaded him to try an experiment. The next day after setting up the field for practice, the coach and I stayed concealed in the groundsman's hut. The players arrived to find the field ready but no coaches. After about 10 minutes of kicking balls around, the players grew restless. Just when the coach was about to intervene, a strong Irish voice called out: 'Let's just get on with it. What if you take the warm-up, David? I will start planning the session'.

The coach had found his leader and learned a valuable lesson. Player-leaders don't emerge unless coaches offer the space that encourages leadership moments to happen.

Too many coaches, insecure and anxious, deny that space by overcoaching and overtraining. When a coach understands that he or she must trust the players on game day, it follows that trust must be part of practice. Table 4.2 illustrates a what-if exercise that

Why Players Won't Lead

Being embarrassed

Not wanting to be different

Frightened of the challenge

Fearing failure

Being unused to responsibility

Stuck in a comfort zone

Afraid of the coach

Can't see the rewards

TABLE 4.2   Leadership Moments Exercise (With Example Responses)

Leadership moment	Victim response	Fighter response
1. We go a goal down after only five minutes of play.	We will lose now.	We have lots of time left to bounce back.
2. We lose a key player to injury.	Our performance will dip.	Great opportunity for a substitute, and I will work harder.
3. The weather and the field are awful.	Nobody can play in these conditions.	We are the best team at dealing with this.
4. We are falling behind in the league.	It's too late to recover.	Every team will have a bad spell—keep fighting.
5. It's getting very tough.	I can't cope.	We do tough.

coaches can use. Player responses stimulate discussion on leadership and help identify potential leaders.

When Phil Jackson, former coach of the Los Angeles Lakers basketball team, found himself with a leaderless team, he stopped calling time-outs. Instead of always looking to the coach for solutions, the team had to find their own. Leadership emerged along with a mentally stronger and more self-managing team. What coach Jackson knew was that

- players may see things during games that coaches are not picking up,
- in some game situations players are themselves best placed to make decisions,
- when players make decisions, their level of commitment to the outcome increases and
- overreliance on the coach can hinder player development and permit easy excuses when things go wrong.

More and more coaches are seeing themselves in the role of supporting their teams rather than commanding them.

Shared Ownership

Shelley Smith, in her conference championship year as head coach of the University of South Carolina women's soccer team, created trust and leadership in a three-stage process.

She started the season being highly directive and insisting on the non-negotiables that she knew were key to any successful team. Then, when she trusted her team, she moved to a far less directive role, encouraging them to take responsibility but staying ready to help. Finally, with trust, responsibility and leadership firmly in place, Shelley was able to allow her team full ownership of the journey. This freed them up to lead themselves to the conference championship.

Shelley found that sharing ownership by encouraging players to lead gave improved team production (increasing commitment to the task) and developed team relationships (building confidence and better communication). This was a winning combination!

> ## Leadership
>
> To lead people, walk beside them.
> People do not notice the best leader.
> The next best, people honour and praise.
> The next, people fear
> And the next, people hate.
> When the best leader's work is done, the people say, 'We did it ourselves'.
> When the effective leader has worked, the people say, 'It happened naturally'.
>
> Lao Tzu (600 BC)

The clear lesson is that a culture of shared ownership encourages player leadership to emerge where

- all players are responsible for their actions,
- team responsibilities are clearly defined,
- coaches give their team freedom to take responsibility,
- no blaming is allowed,
- coaches ask questions and share ownership,
- coaches trust players,
- coaches forgive mistakes made during the learning process,
- coaches give leadership opportunities,
- coaches do not talk about 'my' team but 'our' team and
- coaches reinforce and reward leadership.

Given the environment just described, player leadership should emerge either individually (a captain, an inspirational player, an emotional leader) or in a small group (a core of several players who seize the opportunity to lead). Many of the teams I support have formed leadership groups. A small group of players, usually seniors, are able to act as an effective forum for the coach to discuss issues affecting the team. The leadership group are then able to influence the wider squad.

'How Did We Do?' Exercise

This simple and efficient exercise can be completed in just 10 minutes in the locker-room the first time the team meet after a game. The coach prepares the table (in the recent example I observed) and asks the players to score each section out of 10 (10 high, 5 average, 0 disaster). Space is created for team ownership and a positive discussion, allowing leaders to emerge.

1. Performance Assessment

	Attitude	Defence	Attack	Transition	Set pieces	Discipline
10						
9					✓	
8	✓					✓
7			✓			
6						
5		✓		✓		
4						
3						
2						
1						
0						

(The coach marks each column at the agreed score.)

2. Performance Work-Ons

After the profile is completed, the strengths and weaknesses of the game performance are clear. Coaches can then discuss with the team which of these they should work on in practice before the next game. Ideally, these should be limited to three work-on items.

- Work-on 1:_____
- Work-on 2: _____
- Work-on 3: _____

Team Captains

One of the benefits of experience is that you develop instincts; you can tell when things aren't quite right. Manchester United were preparing to play West Ham, and I wasn't alone in sensing that the team weren't ready. The coaching staff weren't surprised when West Ham scored first after just four minutes. I followed my usual practice of intently watching the reaction of our team.

In a moment like this, even the most dominant coaches are generally helpless. They need to have an inspirational captain and leader on the field. In the short period between the goal and the restarting of the game (when players choose between victim and fighter mentality), the captain Roy Keane made eye, verbal or physical contact with every member of his team. This powerful reminder of each player's responsibility galvanised the team to action. Attitudes changed, and so did performance. The team quickly equalised and went on to win by a large margin.

© Javier Gracia/BPI/Icon Sportswire

Team captains lead on the field.

Which Player-Leader to Choose as Captain?

Coaches might consider selecting their captain on three criteria: talent, attitude and values. Which of these three players would you choose?

Player	Talent (grade)	Attitude (grade)	Values (grade)
1.	A	A	C
2.	A	A	B
3.	B	A	A

Note: Player 3 was not chosen, but he later went on to captain a senior team!

Coaches can work to create a degree of certainty during the game by meticulous preparation. Competitive sport, however, is full of surprises. The captain is the leader on the spot when quick decisions and new direction are needed.

The following list shows the key responsibilities of a captain or leader (where possible, supported by seniors):

- Model the agreed team behaviour.
- Be respected above being liked.
- Communicate with everybody and stimulate discussions.
- Manage the locker-room.
- Understand what the coach is trying to achieve.
- Ensure that group goals are accepted.
- Challenge teammates to raise the bar.
- Be optimistic yet stay realistic.
- Build relationships with everybody.
- Be good at handling conflict and setbacks.
- Be a leader even when not playing well.

This is a big ask for a young man or woman, but I remind potential leaders, 'It's not what you get from sport but who you become'. Captaincy offers the chance to build a wonderful

Questions for a Prospective Captain

1. Are you in control of yourself?
2. Do you want to be liked or respected?
3. Do you understand the team's vision and goals?
4. Do you have a working relationship with every member of the squad?
5. Are you a good model?
6. Can you communicate effectively?
7. Are you composed under pressure?
8. Do you have a good relationship with the coach?
9. Can you challenge your teammates to be better?
10. Are you willing to take charge?

set of skills that are transferrable to almost every other role in life—a valuable opportunity for those brave enough to take it on.

The issue that most often concerns captains or leaders is handling conflict. My advice to them is to do the following:

- Wait for the emotion to die down.
- Establish the facts.
- Assess what is best for the team.
- Try to create a win-win situation.
- Negotiate the solution or compromise.
- Ensure that relationships are not harmed.
- Keep the communication ongoing.
- Move on!

Getting the Right Captain: A Guide for Coaches

Recruit character as well as talent.

Make captaincy an important position.

Discuss and agree what is expected.

If necessary, have two or three co-captains.

Explain to the team the importance of a captain.

Allow space for captains to lead.

Ensure that the captain stays in good relationships with the team.

Help the captain understand team mood and the key signs of change.

Explain how best to handle conflict.

Respect your captain in front of the team.

Always support your captain.

Reward your captain whenever possible.

Always be preparing the next captain—plan for succession.

Being a Model Leader as Coach

The leadership characteristics and style of the coach create the conditions that allow player leadership to emerge. How the coach looks, what she or he says and how she or he acts send powerful messages to the players. The coach must be secure enough to allow space for player leadership to emerge and not be threatened by it. It could be said that coaches get the player-leaders they deserve!

Through intelligent use of power, authority, personality and presence, the coach is able to create a tight yet loose environment. A framework of control is established that includes a small number of non-negotiables (tight) yet enough negotiable (loose) aspects remain to allow player-leaders to shape large parts of the process. This move to increased player ownership is an important part of coaching the modern team.

The coach must always set the standard by personal behaviour, being confident and optimistic, seeing challenges not problems and focusing on what the team can do, not what they cannot do. Communication is especially important. Coaches must ask great questions and listen at least as much as they speak.

SELECTING LEADERS THROUGH PLAYER OWNERSHIP

Lucy and Katy, co-coaches of a successful girls U18 team, worry a great deal about captaining and leadership. In my work with them we have clearly established that women bond to battle and that social cohesion (a sense of family, togetherness and inclusion) is the starting point for their team building.

Although this sense of family is a real strength in their team, it does not help them in their quest to find the captains and leaders they need to trust with on-field decisions. Few female players desire to stand out from their social support group.

Lucy, Katy and I agreed on the following action plan:

1. The coaches would create a lot of space in practice and games so that the players would be forced to take more responsibility.

2. We would look for the girls with the personality, presence and mental toughness to be leaders.

3. The coaches would constantly point out that uncertainty on the field at crucial times would limit success.

4. The team and coaches would meet, and I (a neutral friend) would explain how team leadership relates to team achievement.

5. Everybody would brainstorm the options available for captaincy (no names at this stage) and decide on possible solutions.

6. The team would select three representatives to meet the coaches.

7. At the meeting between the three selected player representatives and coaches, names and solutions would be discussed. At this point the coaches would have the opportunity to safeguard the process from possible damage to the team.

8. The player representatives would then report back to the team.

9. Everybody would meet, finalise the decision and agree to support the chosen captain or captains.

This process requires a lot of discussion and time, but the payback is that the team own the decision and therefore support it, which encourages potential leaders to step up and take responsibility.

Part II

RELATIONSHIPS

A winning team mindset is empowered by the strength of positive relationships within and around the team.

Chapter 5

FORMING BONDS

Soccer is a team game that requires the constant interaction of a number of players under pressure and fatigue. The glue that holds a team together is the players' commitment to the task and their commitment to each other. The strength of their relationships, the bonds formed by practicing and playing together and sharing both good and bad experiences, is tested every game.

I like to demonstrate the power of team bonding by asking a player to snap 11 pencils bound together. Breaking the pencils is very difficult, and the player usually fails. Then I produce four pencils bound together, then three and finally two. Eventually, the player snaps the pencils (usually at two), and the team cheer! The point is clearly demonstrated, especially with younger players, that a whole team bound together are difficult to break, but one or two players isolated from the security of the team are vulnerable.

When coaches begin their careers they naturally focus on the physical, technical and tactical output of their players. But the more experienced coaches appreciate the role of team chemistry and the importance of the team-bonding process. It is a significant moment when a coach realises that success is about 'human beings' as well as 'human doings'.

The highly successful basketball coach Phil Jackson celebrates his career success in his book *Eleven Rings*, but he subtitles it *The Soul of Success*. As Jackson (2013, p 84) says, it is through the forming of team bonds that the soul of the team is developed:

> Basketball is a great mystery. You can do everything right. You can have the perfect mix of talent and the best system of offense in the game. You can devise a fool-proof defensive strategy and prepare your players for every possible eventuality. But if the players don't have a sense of oneness as a group, your efforts won't pay off. And the bond that unites a team can be so fragile, so elusive.

Soccer is full of examples of teams constructed without soul who fail badly against teams with less talent who are bonded together as one.

At the start of the 2014–2015 Premier League season, the champions, Manchester City, lost at home to Stoke City. The difference in talent was much in Manchester City's favour, but the difference in togetherness favoured Stoke. They played not only with each other but for each other, and this attitude released an emotional power that led to a 1-0 victory against all the odds.

This sense of oneness is crucial to successful team soccer performance. Players train and play better when they are happy, and they play tougher when they are playing for each other. Gary Neville, an outstanding player for Manchester United in a successful period, admitted his major motivation and driving force was 'not letting my teammates down'.

The modern coach seeks to build a more powerful team by establishing and generating a strong relationship culture—coach to coach, coach to players, player to player. This arrangement releases the power of human emotion; players are not playing with each other, but for each other. All players give effort, but inspired players find another level of effort—discretionary effort that can be the difference between an adequate performance and a great performance. FC Barcelona is a wonderful example: 'People see Barcelona not as an industry, not as a business, more as a feeling. As a human being you prefer to be involved with a feeling or an emotion than a business', said Barcelona president Sandro Rosell (Wilson 2011a, p 57).

Importance of Relationships

When working with a team, I am happy to let them offer subjects for discussion. Teddy Sheringham, a former Manchester United star, once suggested happiness because he thought that many players did not understand what happiness truly was. After some research I gave a presentation based on the three keys of happiness:

1. Purpose—having compelling direction in your life
2. People—being surrounded by loving relationships
3. Place—a feeling that you are in the right place to live your life

As I expected the discussion that followed reinforced that Manchester United at that time was a happy place to play soccer. What really struck me, though, was the emphasis that the players placed on the importance of people and relationships. Although a few players, especially at the highest levels, can stand alone, the vast majority of the players described their need for the support of teammates and staff.

Establishing Team Bonds

For players to achieve their best for the team, their individual needs must first be met. Identifying those needs is key to the art of modern coaching. Although this statement is true for both men and women, I have consistently found a greater need for personal communication, empathy and supportive relationships in women's soccer teams.

For three years I supported Coach Arjan Veurink in building a successful women's soccer team at FC Twente in Holland. Our starting point was understanding the importance of social cohesion for women players and identifying four key drivers: being needed, being cared for, being appreciated and being listened to.

With these in place, the process of persuading the players to change from a personal agenda to a team agenda can begin. When the players are persuaded of the value of co-operation and collaboration, bonds between players will begin to form.

At first such bonds will be formal and created by practicing as a squad, as a team or in smaller units. Over time, though, this shared purpose and activity stimulate informal bonding and help relationships develop.

So Arjan and his staff built an environment that was warm and inclusive. Players were seen individually, and each was told why and how she was an important member of the squad. The staff ensured that the players received the best care possible, and any problems were dealt with quickly so that players could focus entirely on soccer. This approach also ensured that no excuses could be offered for poor performance. The coaches made a point of emphasising the positives in every situation and constantly showing the women that their effort was appreciated. Finally, Arjan created opportunities for the players to be listened to, individually and collectively, and feel real ownership of their team and their journey.

Football Isn't Chess

Football isn't chess. Serving as a head coach means more than moving Xs and Os around a board. Chess pieces don't have personalities and egos. They don't break their legs, demand higher salaries or move to other chess sets on transfers. Being a head coach requires knowing more than the physics and mechanics of co-ordinating 11 players on the field.

I've learned that as much as the game is played on the field, there are a lot of things outside the field that are also important to winners—I probably spend a little more time on things that go on in the locker-room, go on off the field, the players, their attitude, their motivations, the chemistry of the team and that kind of thing.

Bill Belichick
Head Coach, New England Patriots

From this supportive environment, a strong and positive relationship structure emerged, evidenced by the increased communication, enthusiasm and energy of the players that, of course, translated into better practice and game performances. The power of this relationship bonding, especially in a women's team, is often the key to the day-to-day mood of the team. Bonding is also the team's protection in the difficult times that all teams face. In season 2013 FC Twente won the first Netherlands-Belgium (BE-NE) Women's League title.

In leadership meetings with the senior players at Derby County FC, I illustrated the power of relationship bonding by diagramming a circle enclosing a number of crosses, each X being a member of the playing squad. This diagram represents the 'circle of safety' for a team and is a useful visual aid to engage the players in questions:

What is the glue (the circle) that keeps us together?

Why is the circle important to winning?

Why might a player step outside the circle?

How might we bring him back inside the circle?

How do we ensure that a new player joins us inside the circle?

What can you do as leaders to keep the circle strong?

Care must be taken before attributing any reasons when a player steps outside the boundary of the team circle. For instance, in Ronald Reng's (2010) analysis of German goalkeeper Robert Enke's battle against depression, he outlines the reasons that Robert isolated himself and eventually committed suicide. Pressure affects players in different ways, and coaches and team leaders must show great empathy to players in trouble.

When encouraging team bonding, coaches should bear in mind several points:

- A winning team mindset is a collective mindset.
- Each player in the team has to change from a 'me' agenda to a 'we' agenda.
- Peer pressure is a powerful influence on individual performance.
- A team mindset is always under pressure.
- The strength of relationships acts as glue to help the team stick together during setbacks.
- The power of bonding is a big argument for stability and continuity and a vital factor in the long-term success of teams.
- A strongly bonded team can create the synergy that makes opponents perceive invincibility.
- Playing soccer is more fun if the team enjoy being together.
- High-performance teams are almost always high-relating teams.
- After talent, trust is the key factor in high-performing teams.

Bonding by Sharing

Clemson University women's soccer head coach Eddie Radwanski inherited a team divided by poor relationships. We devised a meeting to open the wounds. I began by reminding the team of their purpose and stressing the need for honesty. I asked the players and the staff each to prepare four questions (key issues that were affecting them as a team and dominating their conversations) for me to answer. The staff and I left the room, and each group prepared their questions. When we returned the players had written four excellent questions anonymously on the flipchart. The staff then added their four questions. I answered a question from each group in turn, acting as a neutral friend and counsellor, and put difficult issues into a new and more positive context. Both groups agreed they had been listened to, and the team had a new and more positive agenda. Coach Radwanski thought that this exercise was an important moment in re-establishing and reinforcing team bonds.

Coaching Relationships and Productivity

Understandably, coaches initially focus on and feel more comfortable with the tangible elements of performance, such as physical and technical outputs. But as they become more experienced, coaches learn that performance follows attitude, so they also learn to embrace coaching the mental and emotional intangibles.

Task cohesion, which is present when every player understands her or his role and responsibilities, has to be allied to social cohesion and positive relationships, to players wanting to play for each other and their coaches.

The three keys to successful coaching are all interrelated:

1. Understanding strategy
2. Improving production (performance on the field)
3. Building relationships

The changing nature of both the game and the modern player has turned coaches from yellers to sellers, and this approach helps maximise the power of relationships. A clear example of this is the decision taken by Derby County manager Steve McClaren to sit high in the stand during games. His message to the team is one of trust and responsibility. Coaches need to develop the desire and skills to understand their players better so that they can maximise the players' production potential. Table 5.1 shows that relationships and production combine to influence winning.

TABLE 5.1   Production, Relationships and Performance

Production	Relationships	Effect on Performance
Good	Good	Peak performance potential
Good	Poor	Potential to win but little commitment
Poor	Good	Good commitment but lacking ability or cohesion

Therefore, social cohesion, establishing firm and positive relationships, is an important part of the agenda for the modern coach. Coaches will always be judged on the results of their teams. Awareness is knowing that the best results are generated by the emotional power of a team bonded in their desire to play for each other and not willing to let teammates down. Maximum production cannot be delivered without the passion of people working together, a point emphasised by leading social psychologist Daniel Goleman (1995):

> The single most important factor maximising the excellence of a team's product is the degree to which the members were able to create a state of internal harmony—which led them to take full advantage of the talent of their members.

> The internal harmony emphasised by Goleman is most threatened when a player or a small group of players step outside the team circle of safety. Coaches and team leaders need to be proactive in recognising this leakage early and encouraging them back inside the team boundary. If this does not work and the team's harmony, and therefore performance, is declining, then a hard decision to remove the dissenting player or players has to be made. What is best for the team always comes first.

Building Good Team Relationships

My experience from grassroots to elite teams has demonstrated that there is a common process in developing and enabling healthy and productive team relationships. Key steps in this process are listed in this section.

1. Build Rapport With Players
Positive relationships are fundamental to creating both an individual and a team mindset that will drive excellent performance. Rapport, an emotional connection between player and coach, sparks an emotional uplift and a happier mood. Such rapport is built on the skill of empathy:

- Learning how the player and team feel
- Feeling what they feel
- Responding appropriately, such as with compassion to distress

Teammates must play for each other, not just with each other.

Empathy connects people. Even simply paying attention to players helps strengthen the emotional connections. Coaches should review when they last spoke to each player on their team.

Coaches can build rapport by showing empathy in several ways to players who are experiencing anxiety:

- Active listening, full attention and good eye contact—'I hear you.'
- Sharing the feelings expressed—'I sense what you are feeling'.
- Building a sense of positivity—'We can overcome this'.
- Co-ordinating efforts—'This is our action plan'.

Table 5.2 illustrates how coaches can orientate their programme to establish positive relationships and encourage rapport.

2. Agree Collectively on an Exciting Purpose for the Team

Nothing binds a team together more than a worthwhile prize—a reward that is bigger than any individual and can only be achieved together (as discussed in chapter 1). For example, when I worked with the England National Team, the players decided that the rewards available were to represent their country, challenge themselves as players, win the European Nations Cup and win the World Cup. The shared vision is a starting

TABLE 5.2   Positive- and Negative-Relationship Coaches

Positive-relationship coach	Negative-relationship coach
Optimist	Pessimist
Seller	Yeller
Teacher	Driller
Lots of communication	Team ignored
Hard work but fun	Boring work, no fun
Noise and laughter	Silence
Shares ideas and listens	Dictates and is unavailable
Sees what players can do	Sees what players can't do
Empowers players	Disempowers players
Always uses names	Seldom uses names
Praises all players	Praises stars
Focus on excellence	Focus on winning
Deals with mistakes	Reacts to mistakes
Fun to be with	No fun to be with
Success belongs to the team	Success belongs to the coach

point for the team agreeing to work together, encourage each other and accept responsibility for their roles. Gene Harker (2014, p 77) in his book *Leadership Intelligence* underlines the importance of meaning:

> Meaning gives direction and purpose to our lives. It's our 'why'—our reason for getting out of bed in the morning. When we have identified our unique calling, we are able to overcome the difficulties we encounter and, with grit, pursue our commitment and goals.

Coaches must make everybody's contribution to this overarching goal clear because this is an important factor in relationship forming. All coaches tend to do this at the start of the season. The best coaches find reasons to reinforce the message at key moments during the season so that its power never fades.

3. Develop a Tough-Love Coaching Style

Players need to be constantly challenged to drive them out of comfort zones. This approach has to be counterbalanced by a fully supportive coaching environment in which challenge is seen as necessary for learning and does not destroy rapport. Mistakes are simply a part of the trial-and-error learning process unless the adverse reaction of the coach damages the self-esteem and confidence of the players. Good coaching is therefore a balance of toughness and love, and the younger the player is, the more the balance tips towards love.

4. Use Peer Pressure

Almost every player seeks some peer approval or acceptance, so peer pressure is often the best way to bring problem players back into line. The job of the coach is to set the agreed team standards repeatedly and win over more and more players. This critical mass will begin to isolate those not buying in to the team standards. Problem players will often be embarrassed out of their poor behaviour and fall in line.

5. Increase Communication

At the end of a successful season, Derby County FC captain Richard Keogh identified clarity as the key reason for their success because the players knew exactly what the coaches wanted. When communication increases, anxiety decreases. The anxiety of not knowing and not understanding hurts relationships. Whenever the mood of the team seems to have changed from positive to negative and relationships are breaking down, some form of communication needs to be initiated, often a team meeting, to get everybody back on the same positive page.

The Player-Centred Coach

Challenges players but supports them as people

Is a teacher, not a critic

Believes in all players and shows it

Focuses on teaching and lets the wins happen

Always shares the credit

Listens more than speaks

Gives players room to grow

Sees defeat as a lost opportunity, never personally

Never shouts or swears

Seeks and takes the advice of others

Is great to work for and always a good friend

Never says 'me', always 'we'

Is part of a team, not apart from the team

With modern technology it is possible to keep in touch 24/7/365. Coaches therefore have a wonderful opportunity to communicate regularly and shape the thinking and feelings of the team. Because the modern player has the right to a point of view, the coach should both ask more questions and arrange regular opportunities for the players to speak and the coaches to listen. The coach must also be aware, when speaking to the media, that his or her comments are now in the public domain and thus could affect team mindset.

6. Be Optimistic But Realistic

One of the greatest qualities of good coaches is their ability to make players and teams believe they are better than they think they are. This climate of optimism brings players together and reinforces relationships: 'If the coach believes, we believe'. Players want to play for an optimistic yet realistic coach who coaches to win, not to avoid defeat. A pessimistic coach displays fear in body language and communication and passes this on to the players. When fear is present, relationships begin to break down.

7. Deal With Emotions

Soccer is a game of emotions as well as thoughts and behaviour. All players are susceptible to their emotional state, whether it is anxiety over their personal game or concerns about the team. Coaches must learn to deal with these emotional ups and downs in a way that does not damage

Teammates must look after each other when emotions are running high.

Building Trust

At times you're not just competing against the opposition; you're fighting everyone else around you to help your team. Comments and behaviours from others are out of our control as coaches. What is in our control is what filters down to the players, how it affects you as a coach, how you protect your team and fight for them, believe in them. This is where trust is built. They have to know you are prepared to fight for them. Then you have a situation where the players will do the same for you. They will want to learn and develop with your help.

Anthony Hudson
Head Coach, New Zealand National Men's Soccer Team

relationships. One of my roles when supporting a head coach is to spot early changes in the emotional state of players or the team. Then coaches need to act quickly and discuss with the team possible reasons for such a change and ways to deal with it.

When a Derby County FC player got sent off for two yellow cards, his emotions prevented him from understanding the referee's actions. Paul Winstanley, former head of analysis at Derby, prepared a clever film that compiled all the incidents throughout the game involving the player that caused the referee to take action. Only when the manager took the player through the film in the calm of the meeting room did the player finally accept responsibility and accountability.

8. Continuity and Stability

Relationships are built over time and through shared experience. Teams with continuity of coach and players are best placed to benefit from the emotional power created between players when strong relationships have been built over time. Constant change of personnel undermines all teaching progression and both task and social cohesion. Many coaches see change as the solution to team difficulties, but often the best answer is to hold their nerve and allow the present team to absorb the learning and begin to produce.

Table 5.3 gives coaches a useful checklist for assessing and improving team relationships. This can be a revealing exercise when undertaken by separate members of the coaching (and support) team and then compared and discussed.

TABLE 5.3   Improving Team Relationships

Statement	Three ways we can improve our team
The team know exactly what their short- and long-term goals are.	1. 2. 3.
Team members freely express real views and are listened to.	1. 2. 3.
All team members have a clear understanding of their roles on the team.	1. 2. 3.
Everyone gets the opportunity to contribute his or her best.	1. 2. 3.
Team members respect and encourage each other.	1. 2. 3.
All relationships in and supporting the team are constructive.	1. 2. 3.
When possible, decisions are by consensus rather than imposed.	1. 2. 3.
Team members are always kept informed of what's going on.	1. 2. 3.
There is little unproductive bickering on the team.	1. 2. 3.
All achievements are recognised and celebrated.	1. 2. 3.

A NEW COACH BUILDS A RELATIONSHIP WITH HIS TEAM

When Coach Paul was appointed the new coach of a senior semi-professional team, he asked for my advice. As a first-time coach who was not a former player, Paul felt anxious about his credibility with the squad. His key question concerned building trust with his new team. I outlined the concept of social capital, the amount of trust and co-operation that a player, the team, or the squad will willingly give the leader, and explained that it is built or destroyed every day by the coaches.

In this context, three factors were crucial for the coach to establish trust:

1. Credibility—is the coach making me and the team better?
2. Reliability—is the coach consistently committed?
3. Empathy—does the coach really care for me and the team?

Paul and I decided on the following programme to build social capital.

- Plan, prepare and be knowledgeable—players will respect a coach who can take them where they want to go.
- Inspire, persuade, communicate—build rapport with each player.
- Agree a value system—establish a basis of trust between players and coaches.
- Be emotionally stable—do not let mistakes or setbacks destroy trust.
- Challenge but support—drive production but offer lots of personal support.
- Be yourself—allow your personality and humour to create an enjoyable working environment.
- Be consistent—do not change the script every day or week.
- Be honest—players need to know you will be honest even when giving them bad news.
- Be patient—don't rush, overcoach (confusing players) or overtrain (wearing players down).
- Be fair—don't treat everybody the same but ensure an essential fairness of approach.

Paul, a serious learner, followed this programme and built a reserve of social capital with his new squad. He was so successful at this that he was forgiven the odd coaching mistake and maintained the goodwill of his squad even when they faced serious adversity later in the season.

Chapter 6

FOSTERING COACHABILITY

I once visited my local soccer club, Crewe Alexandra FC, and watched the head coach, Dario Gradi, spend an hour teaching 10-year-old boys the skills of turning on the ball to lose a defender or open up another part of the field. Dario was very good, but what impressed me most was the coachability of the players, who showed a real appetite to learn. Every player was engaged, focused and actively attempting to master the skill challenge.

Crewe are famous for being a small club who consistently develop soccer players who go on to play at the Premier League and international level. Dario emphasises coachability as the key to sustained progress with players from the age of eight onwards. To succeed at Crewe, players must be

- passionate to get to the next level,
- able to listen and take advice,
- motivated to change and improve,
- strong enough to deal with constructive criticism,
- willing to leave their comfort zone and
- humble enough to keep learning.

Coachability is a key characteristic of every player on the journey to success (see figure 6.1) and vital to the mindset of the modern team. At one time soccer teams could win simply with passion and skill. To that we must now add soccer intelligence—tactical, mental and emotional. Such intelligence can make a team a powerful force, able to dominate games and handle uncertain, unpredictable moments. Coaches everywhere are now under pressure to produce increasingly intelligent players who are high on tactical flexibility, creativity, mental strength and the emotional maturity to cope with all circumstances.

FIGURE 6.1 The player's journey to success.

Arsene Wenger, one of the most intelligent of coaches, highlights his need for intelligent players:

> To be a successful footballer, you must have speed, skills, and eye for goal, the ability to pass, vision and above all the intelligence to put all these aspects into practice. A successful team is calm, patient and intelligent. You win with your intelligence and your brains. (Edwards 2014)

Such a process is dependent on the coachability of players as individuals and team members. Coaches at all levels desire coachable players whose personalities are a good fit for their team. Alongside talent and passion, coachability rates highly in coaches' recruitment criteria, and questions regarding commitment, ability to learn, willingness to adapt and so on must be adequately answered as part of the selection process. Coaches know that being coachable can make an average player good and a good player great.

Being Coachable

Coachability is a key to performance breakthrough for individual players and whole teams. The one essential requirement is the willingness to listen and utilise external input and influences. The extent of this openness to learning determines four levels of coachability:

1. Not coachable—already knows everything, not open, listens only to own voice
2. Selectively coachable—does what's asked but only when he or she feels like it, mostly goes own way
3. Reluctantly coachable—does everything that is asked but doubts it, never fully committed

4. Completely coachable—does everything asked, surrenders own voice, trusts and empowers the coach

Players and teams who reject coaching often believe certain myths:

- Coaching is for beginners.
- We already know everything—we just need to apply it.
- Experienced players coach themselves.

Gareth Barry, a Premier League player at Aston Villa, Manchester City and then Everton FC, was asked to fulfil a number of roles in the midfield of the England team to complement the particular skills of either Steven Gerrard or Frank Lampard. In my opinion Gareth's coachability became key to the team's performance. His character and maturity were evidenced by an ability to listen, a willingness to try new things, an ability to adapt to change and the strength to accept accountability.

Photo courtesy of FC Twente.

Top coaches demand coachable players.

The Coachable Player

Humble
Respectful
Loves the game
Stays in control
Takes responsibility
Thinks long term
Keen to learn
Excited by change
Willing to try new things
Unafraid of mistakes
Not hung up on the past
Inquisitive
Trusts coaches

Of course, Gareth made mistakes, but he freely admitted them, took responsibility for them and rarely made the same mistake again.

How players adapt to coaching says a great deal about who they are. The same is true of teams. Coachability is an aspect of team mind-set. Progress depends on the commitment of all individual members to learn their team roles and responsibilities. Great coaches can win with less talent but only if the team have a high level of coachability (see table 6.1). The New England Patriots of the American NFL have been Super Bowl winners and a dominant force in the league under the guidance of their outstanding coach, Bill Belichick, who recruits coachability:

> Belichick's system relies heavily on smart, adaptable players. The intellectually rigorous, team-centric Patriots system would flop without smart, selfless, passionate players. Belichick's previous club played the same system but failed because many players weren't coachable. The Patriots have acquired many superb players who achieved little on other teams that did not utilise those players' intelligence and adaptability.
>
> Belichick's staff relentlessly squeezes maximal performance from players whose 'excellence' is defined by their heads and hearts as much as their arms and legs. (Lavin 2005, p 53)

Being coachable is important at all ages and levels of competition. All coaches have limited time to teach the skills of soccer, so they rely on players to be early for practice; ready, fresh and alert; keen to learn and determined to excel.

Superstars Have Coachability

When Steve Round, the former assistant manager of Manchester United, walked out for his first practice session with his new squad, he was a little nervous. Coaching superstars is daunting, and he was still unsure of the right approach. However, one of the senior players walked alongside him and told him how much the players were looking forward to the session. He went on to add that the players loved being challenged to learn new things. The word was that 'Roundy' and the manager, David Moyes, were demanding coaches. A valuable lesson learned—many superstars are highly coachable and need to be challenged every day!

TABLE 6.1 **Assessing Your Team's Coachability**

Rate each answer on a scale of 1 to 5.

Score 1: Disagree with the statement

Score 5: Completely agree with the statement

Our team	1	2	3	4	5
1. Want to learn					
2. Are unafraid of change					
3. Listen attentively					
4. Enjoy and engage in practice					
5. Respect the coaches					
6. Take responsibility for mistakes					
7. Respond well to instruction from the coaches					
8. Communicate openly with the coaches					
9. Do not get angry when criticised					
10. Are determined to master skills and tactics					
11. Relate well to each other					
12. Are open to new ways of trying things					
13. Recover well from mistakes and setbacks					
14. Do not make excuses					
15. Do not complain					
16. Trust the coaches' expertise					
17. Respond well to honest feedback					
18. Accept ownership of the performance					
19. Always display a positive attitude					
20. Contribute suggestions for improvement					
Assessment (general guidance only): 100–80 = high coachability 79–60 = average coachability 59–0 = low coachability					

Being Uncoachable

The world's most brilliant coach would fail without players who are willing and able to learn from her or him. I saw Paul Barron, a goalkeeping coach responsible for the development of many fine goalkeepers, fail with only one goalkeeper. This particular player had had some early success before Paul joined his club. From the start the player rejected Paul's coaching and experience, insisting that he knew best how to prepare. The other goalkeepers in the squad responded well to Paul, and it was no surprise when one of them accelerated through to win the first-team jersey, leaving behind a talented but uncoachable failing star.

Unfortunately, coaches, especially of younger players, are encountering more players who are uncoachable. Some players believe they are never wrong, others think that the coach picks on them unfairly, and, of course, some will not take responsibility for mistakes or failure. These instances of uncoachable behaviour reflect various forms of mental or emotional weakness:

- Arrogance
- Indifference—doesn't care
- Anger—instantly fights back
- Subversion—finds victim 'friends'
- Low self-esteem:
  - Unwilling because afraid
  - Makes assumptions and avoids accountability
  - Being wrong, when this is associated with feeling of less worth
  - Takes everything personally
  - Worries about things he or she cannot control

The moment that determines whether a player or team are coachable or uncoachable is immediately after a coach intervenes with advice, instruction or criticism. Figure 6.2 illustrates the choice for the player or team between responding positively and reacting negatively. From the first moment a young boy or girl starts to learn soccer, that choice reflects the person's character and determines his or her soccer destiny, unless a coach at some point can influence a change from negative to positive.

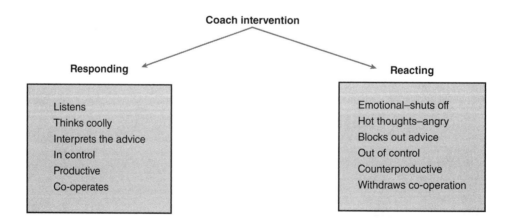

FIGURE 6.2 Responding or reacting to coach intervention—a measure of coachability.

Developing Coachability

Coachability is a function of the following factors:

1. The player's motivation to learn and improve
2. The player's desire to achieve her or his goals and dreams
3. The strength of the relationship between the player and the coach

For the team we must add these points:

4. Trust in others to do their jobs
5. Open and honest communication
6. Open and clear expectations of each other

Ensuring player and team coachability is about shaping these thoughts and emotions positively. This notion goes beyond physical, technical and tactical instruction and engages the coach more as a psychologist and relationship builder. Of course, the coach's job is to challenge players to improve, but if these elements of coachability are not in place, no learning will occur. Basketball coach Phil Jackson had to coach the uncoachable LA Lakers, star players who had lost any sense of humility and gone backwards from a 'we' attitude to a 'me' attitude. The lesson he shared was this: 'The essence of coaching is to get the players wholeheartedly to agree to being coached, then offer them a sense of their destiny as a team' (Jackson 2013, p 17).

Coach Jackson convinced his players that the only way to win was by being willing to be coached as one cohesive team unit.

Fully developed coachability means players become self-managing and take responsibility for their own learning. This is the mindset of a champion player or team. They come to learn every day and never waste a practice. I recommend that players engage in a 12-step programme to develop self-management:

1. Take responsibility and make no excuses.
2. Decide whether you want to be a fighter or a victim.
3. Set an achievement journey.
4. Plan targets for each day.
5. Define your own job description.
6. Profile your own strengths and weaknesses.
7. Build a disciplined routine.
8. Manage your own time and energy.
9. Learn something every day.
10. Don't get in your own way.
11. Accept that you are accountable.
12. Never give in!

Martin Krag on the website bundesligafanatic.com (2012) gave a fascinating insight into William Kvist, a top Danish international soccer player who is dedicated to self-managing his coachability:

> William Kvist is a true professional and his approach to football is similar to the one you'll find in individual sportsmen like triathletes or swimmers. He takes responsibility for his own development in a world where players are used to being taken care of and catered to as long as they get themselves to the training ground and to the stadium on match days. Kvist himself calls it the hunt for perfection and that's why he has surrounded himself with a team of psychologists, hypnotherapists, dieticians and mental coaches.
>
> 'I didn't become a true professional before I took responsibility for my own development and started to train on my own with the help from my team of practitioners. I had a contract but didn't behave like a professional. That came when I started to focus on my weaknesses. What I didn't get at the training ground I worked on myself, and the improvement followed,' says Kvist.
>
> In the team bus on match days you'll find Kvist at the back with headphones on and closed eyes listening to the voice of his mental coach telling him that he will control the midfield, that he will dominate and own the centre of the field. And in the car on his way to the training ground Kvist will be listening to classical music because the radio commercials are disturbing his concentration.

William Kvist is a good example of a highly coachable and self-managing player. Every coach should encourage this mindset in young players. It begins with creating a practice and game environment where learning is encouraged and rewarded. At first the players must be shown the ways in which they can improve their performance, though eventually, like Kvist, they should be able to develop intrinsic motivation and be allowed to take control over their own learning.

Creating a Learning Environment

In my experience many of the barriers to learning and being coached are removed by creating a healthy and productive environment as a foundation upon which to build. Such an environment is the sum total of everything that affects the player's psychological and emotional well-being and therefore has a direct or indirect influence on performance. Coaches create a learning environment by making learning a key objective of performance. Because soccer is learned through trial and error, coaches must create a zone of psychological safety that fosters change and innovation and, more important, removes the fear of being embarrassed by making mistakes. Fear can stifle the learning process and prevent the development of those valuable players who can think outside the box.

Coaches remove fear and encourage new learning with a tough and warm coaching style that challenges but always stays in tune with each player's and the team's feelings.

The coaching environment is important because the coach has control over it and determines whether it is a positive, productive place to learn soccer or not. Many of the mental and emotional strengths that players gain are achieved through daily exposure to a challenging but positive and productive coaching environment. This sort of setting enables players to maximise their talent potential. Because the programme is well prepared and organised, nothing detracts from quality teaching time. Enthusiastic coaches teach mastery of the skills and constantly stress excellence in performance rather than focus on results. Players are given individual learning goals and allowed sufficient learning time every session. Progress is measured and rewarded. Effort is constantly recognised and praised, and the player receives continual feedback, especially after making mistakes.

The most effective leaders always explain why a skill is being taught and what benefits it will bring. They think and act positively, spreading optimism and a can-do attitude. From careful observation they offer the players accurate, objective and supportive feedback. Tolerance of mistakes is part of the learning process, and the good coach is able to interpret such failures as learning moments.

Of great importance is using games as an important learning experience, as a test of development rather than simply a win or a loss. All learning progress in practice can be destroyed by a results-fixated coach at game time. The best coaches do their best teaching at game time.

Establishing Work Standards

Understand exactly what work is required.

Ensure that all work is relevant to the age, gender and competitive level of the players.

Always explain why the work is needed.

Communicate your high expectations.

Encourage all players to work to their maximum potential.

Establish hard work as a team ethic.

Model the high standards you set.

Do not accept mediocrity.

Reward good work.

Building Resonance

Key to creating a learning environment is removing fear and building the psychological stability that allows continual progress. Players are encouraged to become better players, but they need to feel secure in the environment to get the best out of themselves.

The aim is a state of resonance, a seamless fit between how players want to feel and how the coaching environment allows them to feel. In competitive sport a battle occurs every day between positives (creating resonance) and negatives (creating dissonance).

Table 6.2 shows a simple way of involving players (or staff or parents) in a shared exercise to build a resonant environment suitable for their team.

Coaches must focus on what makes their coaching situation healthy for the players and safeguard it against all threats by developing their own emotional intelligence. Such coaches demonstrate empathy by wanting to help their team develop with a minimum of frustration and disappointment. They build their emotional intelligence by tuning into what they themselves are thinking and feeling and what their team members are thinking and feeling. Martyn Newman (2007), an expert on emotional intelligence describes the benefits: 'Empathy creates and maintains happy, productive relationships by focusing on the whole person—not just tasks—and creates reserves of emotional capital that can be drawn on when the pressure is on'.

TABLE 6.2   Ensuring a Resonant Environment

EXERCISE: IN LIST AND OUT LIST, NO NAME REQUIRED	
We need to create a winning environment. Decide what things should be in for us as a team—things that make you feel good, feel more positive, give you greater energy and so on—and put them in the in list. Decide what things should be out for us as a team—things that upset you, make you anxious or negative and reduce your energy—and put them in your out list.	
In	**Out**
1.	1.
2.	2.
3.	3.
4.	4.
5.	5.
6.	6.
7.	7.
8.	8.
9.	9.
10.	10.

A soccer coach who is both soccer smart and people smart will build a resonant learning environment, a positive emotional climate that frees the best in players and gets a high-energy and fully engaged performance. Emotions are contagious, and the emotional effect of what the coach says or does is crucial. The more emotionally demanding the learning and work are, the more empathy and support the coach needs to show.

> I've learned that people will forget what you said, people will forget what you did, but people will never forget how you made them feel.
>
> Maya Angelou
> Poet, actor and civil rights activist

The take-away message from this quotation is that coaches must not ignore how their players are feeling if they want them to engage fully in absorbing and assimilating new information and skills. Only when players are tuned in emotionally will they tune in properly to the coaching process. Coaches have an opportunity to create such resonance when they interact with their team by starting with the question, 'How is everyone feeling today?'

Adopting an Appropriate Coaching Style

The most important relationship in soccer is that of the coach and the player. When this relationship is positive and strong, the coachability of the player increases.

Many of the present generation of young players have been raised with a different attitude to work and commitment. Each generation has its own difficulties, and the challenge for the coach is to find a way to engage young people to learn the game, be willing to be coached and work hard to achieve success. Good coaches find the most suitable coaching style for their particular team.

Chris Panayiotou, developmental director of coaching at Virginia Rush Soccer Club (previously at

My Favourite Coach

My favourite coach growing up as a young teenager was also our school's English teacher. He was so passionate and cared about the game, it was infectious. But what stood out and made me like and respect him was that he had these strange, quirky little gestures and facial expressions—all centred on getting his point across. Whether it be talking to you about a block tackle or encouraging you after a disappointing game—he was passionate. And he was funny. But most of all, he was himself and that endeared others and me towards him. That authenticity has stuck with me and has given me everlasting fond memories of my time as a young footballer.

Anthony Hudson
Head Coach, New Zealand National Men's
Soccer Team

Rush Wisconsin), created a practice and playing environment that constantly encouraged his U12 team to develop

- as successful players who enjoy learning, make progress and achieve,
- an understanding of the basic principles of play,
- as confident players who are able to play in a variety of positions and
- as responsible citizens who make a positive contribution to society and soccer.

Chris sums up his philosophy:

> What we do need to know is many of us are making a difference in many children's lives whether they go to play at the highest level or their highest level. Children never forget a good teacher. It is my goal never to be anyone's last coach.

Coaches themselves can be a barrier to learning if their style turns off the players. An inspirational leader like Chris is often all that is needed to turn around a failing soccer team. To encourage learning in their players, coaches should demonstrate the following characteristics:

- Be clear on how they want the team to play.
- Encourage shared ownership with the team.
- Seek to inspire.
- Sell, not yell.
- Communicate constantly.
- Encourage player input.
- Teach, teach, teach!
- Be helpful and approachable.
- Focus on the process, not the outcome.
- Measure and reward progress
- Deal with setbacks well—assign no blame.
- Be fun to be with.

Criticising the Team and Getting a Positive Response

1. Don't meet until the emotion has died down.
2. Remind the team of their agreed goals.
3. Praise the team for the goals they have already met.
4. Specify the goals not being met.
5. Produce the objective evidence (film never lies).
6. Share perceptions—point out how others see them.
7. Ask the team for any input at this stage—'Is this fair?'
8. Stress what will happen if nothing changes.
9. Identify what can change.
10. Set out an action plan for change and improvement.
11. Ask for team input—'Can you commit to this?'
12. Remotivate and end positively with a highlights film, team huddle or other activity.

So the most appropriate coaching style that fosters player coachability is one balanced between challenge and support. Challenging players is important because soccer skills are learned by hard work and frequent repetition of the basics. Getting good performance is possible only if players connect to the work ethic. Champions understand that 'the road to execution is paved with repetition'. Supporting players is equally important. If there is insufficient attention to relationships and the players feel the coach does not care for them, they will engage in soccer with far less enthusiasm and energy.

OVERCOMING RESISTANCE TO COACHING

Coach Tom inherited a team of U15 boys who rejected coaching and had seen the departure of several well-meaning coaches. Tom discussed this with me, and we decided that we needed to change the way the team were thinking and slowly build up coachability. Because of the deep-rooted nature of the resistance, we had to think creatively. We came up with the following programme:

1. For the first three practices Coach Tom was a pleasant guy with a whistle who just let the team play games.

2. A practice game was arranged with a well-coached opponent. When the boys lost 0-4 Tom simply remarked, 'Well, that was fun'.

3. As anticipated, by now a reaction was building from both players and parents, so the coach called a meeting before the next practice.

4. At the meeting 'WHAT DO YOU WANT?' was written on the board. The answer came back that everybody wanted to achieve. So Tom wrote on the board 'WHAT DO WE NEED TO DO?' The answer included being coached to improve. Tom then handed to each player and his parents a sheet containing his eight rules of practice:

    1. Be on time and be ready.
    2. Run when the coach whistles.
    3. Listen attentively.
    4. Try very hard to play as the coach asks.
    5. Help each other to learn.
    6. Respond positively to feedback from the coach.
    7. Be willing to change your game.
    8. Understand that change can be uncomfortable.

When every player and his parents had signed and returned the sheet, Tom continued with practice.

1. Tom did not revolutionise practice, but he slowly integrated short, sharp learning moments within an enjoyable game structure.

2. A visit was arranged for the team and parents to watch a professional team practise. The whole concept of work, focus and coachability was emphasised.

3. A return match with the previous opponents saw the team tie 2-2 and appreciate the improvements they had made.

Tom is now in his third season with the team!

Chapter 7

REQUIRING ACCOUNTABILITY

The great striker Jimmy Floyd Hasslebaink once missed a wonderful scoring opportunity to defeat Arsenal in the last minute of a game. When the locker-room had settled, Jimmy rose to his feet and said to everyone, 'I did not do my job today. I apologise. I will do my job better in our next game'.

Jimmy made himself accountable, moved on and then scored two goals in the next game. He had also set a precedent for the younger players on the team by showing them that taking responsibility is the right thing to do!

A key stage in the development of a collective winning team mindset occurs when everyone in the locker-room accepts accountability for his or her performance. This is a major threshold in terms of relationships, learning, character development and team mental toughness. Players face no greater pressure to perform well than knowing that through their actions they will be accountable to their teammates and coaches.

This stage is not only a key achievement for teams but also marks a decisive moment in the development of a coach. As teams move beyond playing soccer for fun and begin to work on building an attitude to winning competitive games, so also the coach must embrace the requirement for greater accountability. Such accountability is the final stage in a well-planned and delivered coaching process in which coaches are tested on their ability to

- communicate clear player job descriptions,
- plan and deliver a coherent game plan,
- subjectively assess player performances as accurately as possible,
- use valid objective performance data to verify assessments,
- communicate performance shortfalls to individual players or the team in an effective yet nonblaming manner and
- use such teaching moments as a lever for progress and development.

Eric Steele, goalkeeping coach for Derby County FC, has a distinguished record for producing elite goalkeepers. Eric's philosophy is simple—preparation and accountability. Goalkeeping is about attention to detail, and preparation is vital. Of course, mistakes happen, but Eric insists that the best learning is achieved by making his goalkeepers accountable:

> Goalkeeping is a very precise discipline based on preparation and concentration. When this breaks down I need my goalkeepers to be accountable and tell me why it happened. That way they take responsibility and learn so that we reduce the chances of future similar mistakes.

For Eric, these accountability sessions with the goalkeepers are not about blaming but about responsibility and learning. Good play in both practice and games is stressed. With the use of film replay, Eric asks the goalkeeping group to analyse the things that could be done better. Eric believes that the most significant learning takes place when players accept responsibility and determine better solutions for the future. The only time Eric intervenes strongly is when players continually repeat the same mistake.

Accountability is the obligation of a player or team (and, indeed, the coach) to account for their actions and accept responsibility for them. As players and teams rise to higher levels of competition, the level of accountability increases and a real test of character begins. One of the most significant performance anxieties is that of being constantly judged by others, and a strong mindset is needed to deal with the ever-present approval or disapproval of coaches, family, friends, fans and the media.

For team mindset to grow and strengthen, each player and the team as a whole must accept accountability for their performance. Accountability begins by learning in practice what has to be done and then taking responsibility for doing it on game day. This process is linked to trust; the coach prepares the team all week and then trusts them to perform on game day. Coaches have to appreciate that trust works both ways and that they too are accountable for their actions. A mature and wise coach openly takes responsibility for her or his mistakes in front of the team or through the media. This human response is more likely to build trust than destroy it.

Taking Responsibility

Accepting responsibility is a necessary step towards handling accountability. Players are brought together to enable the development of a consistently successful team. Every member of the squad is there for a purpose, has a role to play and therefore has a responsibility to him- or herself, the team and the coaches. The power of a collective mindset rests on the shared understanding that everybody can be trusted to carry out his or her responsibilities. This agreement becomes a strong, sound basis for accepting and dealing with postgame accountability.

This process can be difficult for the millennial generation who are focused on entitlements (or rights) rather than responsibilities. Too many entitlements get in the way of developing resilience and mental toughness.

For that reason the Netherlands club FC Twente has changed their approach with academy players. In their recruiting, the club made the mistake of stressing the entitlements of the player (and family) rather than the responsibilities. This approach led to subsequent behavioural issues. Recently this policy was reversed, and a three-stage process was put into place.

1. Responsibilities—if you join this club you will be expected to . . .
2. Respect—if you carry out your responsibilities you will win our respect.
3. Rights—and then we will ensure that you receive the appropriate benefits.

Each academy coach at every age level is asked to determine eight key responsibilities to teach the players during the season. As players progress they become accustomed to taking responsibility (for instance, I have never seen a coach carrying any equipment), and this easily transforms into being able to accept accountability. Players constantly receive these messages:

- Be where you are supposed to be, when you are supposed to be there.
- Do what you are supposed to do, when you are supposed to do it.
- Do what you say you are going to do.
- Do it for yourself and to help the team.
- Be responsible for your job.
- Be accountable to others. Players who can be trusted get rewarded.

Ten Key Elements of the Accountability Cycle

Taking responsibility and accepting accountability should be woven into the fabric of any soccer club. The following elements are essential to this process.

Players must be held accountable for their actions.

1. Goals and Standards

Coaches and players should collectively agree on team and individual goals and standards that are achievable and appropriate to the age and ability level of the players. Good communication at this stage is vital so that every player is clear on what is expected from her or him. Mike Krzyzewski, the head basketball coach at Duke University, is a coach from whom many soccer coaches can learn. His teams always demonstrate high standards:

> In putting together your standards, remember it is essential to involve your whole team. Standards are not rules issued by the Boss—they are a collective identity. Remember standards are the things you do all the time and the things for which you hold one another accountable.

Involvement in many team sports besides soccer has confirmed to me that good coaches demand a small number of non-negotiables, universal standards that set the tone for individual and team accountability:

timekeeping, appearance, courtesy and respect, commitment, attention, discipline and appropriate lifestyle choices. Beyond these, the team should ideally have involvement in agreeing goals and standards.

2. Reminders

To help players remember their commitments, coaches need to find ways to integrate agreed goals and standards into the everyday life of the club. One coach I work with prints out the agreement and holds a buy-in ceremony (with pizza and parents present) where each player signs up to the commitment. These posters are displayed through the club. When players do not maintain standards, the coach merely has to take the poster into a team meeting and remind them what they signed up to do.

3. Culture

Coaches should try to build a culture throughout the club, staff included, where accepting and taking responsibility is the norm. They should encourage everybody to help each other to meet goals and keep standards. Such a culture would emphasise purpose, standards, responsibility, commitment, flexibility and rewards. NFL coach Brian Billick (2001) stresses the link between accountability and integrity:

> On NFL teams that have integrity, players and coaches are compelled to take personal responsibility for a mistake they might have made in order not to let blame fall elsewhere. Such accountability is a sign of respect. It is a reflection of the team's integrity when individuals take responsibility for their actions.

4. Learning Environment

Attaining goals and standards that have been set is a process that coaches teach and players learn. Every player on the team must be given maximum opportunity to learn and do his or her job to the required standard. Making a mistake, suffering a setback and not taking responsibility are useful teaching moments when real learning can take place. As experienced coaches recognise, teams often have to fail to succeed later. But continual failure to learn and adapt behaviour has to be dealt with before it damages team progress.

5. Accepting Justified Criticism

Coaches have to teach players to understand that a critical appraisal of their performance is honest and well-meaning feedback aimed at improvement. Although listening to the player is an essential part of feedback, coaches can use this opportunity to teach the difference between reasons and excuses. Before responding to any player's account of performance failure, a coach must determine which statements are valid reasons and which are simply excuses for not doing her or his job.

Coach Anson Dorrance, who has an outstanding record in USA women's soccer (Dorrance and Nash 2014), points out that the differences men and women players often show when dealing with criticism:

> For men, you have to use videotape because they won't believe the criticism otherwise. With women, a video is more effective as a tool to show the positive aspects of performance and show them they played well. A lot of women don't have the confidence to feel they are as good as they actually are. It's not that you never show negative aspects of performance to women's teams, but seeing their mistakes on tape doesn't really help them. They believe you when you tell them they made a mistake. A video can almost make it worse because it magnifies the mistake.

6. Regular Feedback

Ensuring a constant flow of accurate feedback so that full accountability for failing behaviour on and off the field does not come as a surprise is another step in making a team accountable. Good coaches instinctively know when a player is struggling, and they should be proactive in confronting the player with early warning feedback, especially if their judgement is supported by performance data. Table 7.1 shows a list of simple performance measurements that can really help a coach in a player feedback session. At a professional level these measures are tracked objectively game by game to show variations in performance.

TABLE 7.1 Ten Key Performance Measurements for Young Players

Activity	Total (as recorded in each game)
Passes received	
Passes made successfully	
Assists leading to shots	
Successful tackles	
Interceptions made	
Headers won	
Shots made	
Shots on target	
Goals scored	
Saves made	

Note: All these can be recorded by volunteers.

7. Thunderbolts

Every team will face the occasional thunderbolt—a completely unexpected setback or defeat. Coaches should accept these happenings as abnormal and move on, not let them affect accountability nor allow them to undermine overall team progress. As soon as possible after such a game, although after emotions have settled down, the coach must switch the team mindset back to the bigger picture. Whilst acknowledging the disappointment of losing, here the coach has to recalibrate the mindset of the team; reaffirm the overall progress the team is making, change feelings from negative back to positive, and set up the expectation of success in the forthcoming games. As discussed in chapter 5, this step is important in building and maintaining good relationships.

8. Internal Challenge

In an ideal competitive and accountable environment, teammates can feel safe to challenge each other when performance goals and standards are not being met. Peer group pressure is a powerful shaper of team and individual behaviour. Players on championship teams hold each other accountable and don't wait for the coach to intervene. To maintain relationships, peer challenges should be given as positive statements of support—'You are better than this', rather than the unhelpful, 'You are rubbish today'.

9. 'Can't Do' or 'Won't Do?'

Before assessing accountability, coaches should ask whether failing behaviour is 'can't do', a physical or technical or tactical problem to be solved on the training ground, or 'won't do', an attitude problem to be resolved in discussion with coaches, parents or a sport psychologist. For example, I was asked to intervene with a fullback who was failing to make the runs required from defence to support the attack. I discovered that he was quite willing to do this but physically could not keep repeating these long runs. This was not a question of 'won't do' (he was willing) but 'can't do' (he needed better physical preparation). Coaches must ask and seek answers to this question before criticising players.

10. Accountability Without Blame

Coaches should ensure that any performance review and subsequent accountability are based on solid information and evidence, not an emotional knee-jerk reaction to a particular incident. The coach must show emotional intelligence in making the review a learning experience that does not damage relationships (discussed more fully later in this chapter). The review should conclude with an agreed action plan to amend and improve performance, and the player should leave the review process in a stronger place mentally (see figure 7.1).

Figure 7.1   Review Questions That Help Players Understand Their Performance Psychologically

- What stressed you at today's match?
- How did you experience that stress (thoughts, actions, body)?
- How did you deal with it?
- How was your self-talk (positive, negative, varied)?
- How was your level of arousal (low, perfect, high)?
  - On the way to the game
  - Warming up
  - During the game
  - At halftime
- What did you learn today that will help in the next game?
- What mental-training techniques were most helpful to you?
- What was enjoyable about today?
- How would you rate your performance? (poor, average, good)
- What do you need to work on?

Building Accountability

If the agreed goal of the team is to work hard, improve and win soccer games, then both players and coaches must be accountable. The higher the competitive level is, the more players will recognise that being held accountable every day will contribute to performing well on game day.

So requiring accountability must be part of any coaching philosophy and style. Coaching is about providing constant challenge with appropriate support, and holding players accountable is tough but necessary. Dave Anderson (2001), a leadership expert, stressed the importance of requiring accountability:

> Leaders must develop a lower threshold for alibis and become better communicators and enforcers of what they want done. If you are more interested in being liked and popular than holding people accountable for results, you have a serious leadership weakness. It's not your job to make people happy. Your job is to get them better. Holding people accountable to high standards and results is nothing to apologise for. Failing to stretch them to their potential is.

Tom Crothers in his biography (2006) of Anson Dorrance, women's soccer coach at the University of North Carolina, explains how Anson created a 'competitive cauldron' to force his players into competitiveness, responsibility and accountability. This system included grading each player for every aspect of practice, building up report cards for each player and regularly posting player rankings on the board for everyone to see. Anson wanted to create competitive intensity in practice and teach the players to accept accountability for their performance every day.

All coaches operate within the limits set by the context of their team (age, gender, level of competition and so on). The context determines the amount and type of accountability to be applied, which varies from the recreational player who just wants to enjoy soccer with friends to the professional player whose performance and accountability is a formal responsibility. Coaches have to learn to judge and apply accountability measures appropriate to their teams.

> Players always want to blame someone else or some circumstance out of their control for their problems. It's an embarrassing state. Many of today's players don't want to be embarrassed, so they spread the embarrassment. The coach didn't play him enough or he didn't get enough shots or he has a banged up finger. You find a way to not accept the blame. The better players learn to say, 'I played bad but tomorrow I'll play better'. A lot of younger players are afraid to admit they have bad nights but everybody has bad nights and it's how you rebound from those bad nights that dictates what kind of player you are going to be.
>
> Michael Jordan

Performance Reviews

Player and team accountability is best maintained by scheduling regular performance reviews. This process is demanding on a coach in terms of time, energy and emotion, and it requires a constant commitment to establishing the facts of each player's performance. If undertaken properly, the task is arduous, but outstanding coaches are willing to make that commitment because the benefits in developing accountability and mutual trust can be huge.

The main challenge in performance reviews is assembling a full and fair picture of each player's contribution. This review will mainly consist of hard evidence—performance statistics (an example of a professional performance profile used in reviews is illustrated in table 7.2) and film clips. Coaches should also use their experience and instinct to provide soft evidence through their own performance observations. The best assessment often comes from the players themselves through insightful questioning by the coach. Without some form of performance review and ongoing accountability, neither the players nor the team are likely to realise their full potential.

TABLE 7.2   Prozone Game Performance Benchmark for a Premier League Attacker (Season Averages 2013–14)

PHYSICAL	Distance covered	10.63 km
	High-intensity distance covered	1,026 m
	High-speed run distance	725 m
	No. of sprints	43
	Recovery time	46 sec
TECHNICAL	Total passes	24.3
	Passing success %	78.1
	Shots	3.0
	Shots on target	1.7
	Crosses	1.2
	Balls received	36.7
	Tackles	16
	Headers	6.7

Source: Prozone Performance Benchmark (extracted from a Premier League Positional Analysis, April 2013-2014).

An objective way of conducting a performance review that does not damage relationships starts with a team meeting that uses filmed game excerpts to demonstrate the good things that the team did and praise positive aspects of play. Following the team session, the coach takes aside individual players and shows each person the parts of her or his performance that were disappointing. Because this session is for teaching rather than blaming, these short one-to-one reviews are a good example of 'eyeball leadership' in action, and they end with points being made without damaging relationships. Praise in public and criticise in private.

Performance reviews provide these benefits:

- Reaffirmation of goals set
- Opportunity to set new goals
- Recognition of good performance
- Clarification of standards expected
- Chance for a coach to influence a player

- Chance for a player to influence a coach
- Rebuilding of trust and making an emotional connection
- Reinforcement of team culture and values
- Motivation of subsequent behaviour

The elements of the review process are obviously influenced by the ability level, age and gender of the players. They may include the following:

- Reviewing progress since the last review
- Outlining the coach's view of the player's contribution using hard and soft evidence
- Listening to the player's perspective
- Agreeing on the future:
  - What can be accomplished?
  - What needs to be done?
- Setting an optimistic tone—'You're not there yet but there's always room to grow'
- The coach thanking the player for his or her continued effort and commitment
- Restating of the agreed action plan, which may be followed up in written form.

The England rugby team meet on at least eight occasions during the year. On each occasion the head coach, Stuart Lancaster, meets every player for a 15-minute performance review. Both Stuart and the players value this highly in both performance and relationship terms.

The international context is unusual, and for most coaches who work with their teams on a daily or weekly basis, it is not relevant. However, performance review can be scaled to match the team situation, and the process should never be ignored. For instance, coach Mike Jolley, when he was working with the Crewe Alexandra U15 team, simply chose one player to walk out to the field with and another player to walk back in with every practice. Mike accomplished two valuable but quick and efficient performance review sessions at every practice. Coach Paul Simpson of Derby County FC uses the bus trips to away games to have players come and sit with him for their performance review chat.

Progress does not occur without feedback and accountability!

INSIDE THE TEAM

MOVING A TEAM TOWARDS ACCOUNTABILITY

Coach Alex had a problem with his U18 boys team. When he tried to evaluate performances the players would not take responsibility, made excuses and blamed each other. The situation had reached such a low point halfway through the season that Alex and I decided to reset the clock and act as if the season were starting anew.

We set out a programme based on four criteria:

1. Maintaining relationships so that the players felt like volunteers, not victims
2. Improving work ethic and focus and emphasising continual improvement
3. Slowly increasing the challenge on the players while offering constant teaching and support
4. Introducing a rolling programme of accountability performance reviews

We explained the programme:

- Alex made clear that the season was to start again.
- All performances would be measured only from this point on.
- The team would set new goals and standards for the rest of the season.
- The team would commit to these goals in a signing ceremony to accepting the challenge. Parents would be invited to witness.
- The signed posters would be placed in prominent positions.
- Individual players would agree on personal targets with the coach.
- Alex clearly set out the direction, work and improvement necessary for the team and each player.
- The team would be graded each week on (1) effort and (2) performance.
- Alex would create both a motivational (emphasising the positive) and learning environment where every player would get the help needed.
- Performance measures available to the coach would be used as objective criteria.
- Performance reviews would become the centre of a rolling programme of coach-player meetings.
- An external coach (me) would review the coach and his staff.

Under the new programme a burst of enthusiasm and energy occurred that led to renewed effort. The squad divided into three groups—those who could be trusted and loved the challenge, those who struggled a little but would always try hard and those who couldn't shake off their habits of making excuses and blaming when made accountable. But team performance, with great parental support and some clever coaching, improved dramatically.

Chapter 8

SYNCHING APTITUDES

Recently I came across an enterprising coach of a boys U16 team who had decided to base his team's game on FC Barcelona's 4-3-3 formation. To excite and stimulate his players, he modelled his team on Barcelona by showing game film of Barcelona in action and having each player identify with his Barcelona counterpart.

After the team were familiar with Barcelona's shape and style of play, the coach personalised each player's role by calling him by the name of the Barcelona player who held the same position. He constantly fed the team images of Barcelona in action; for example, if the team were to practise transition into a counterattack, they would see three examples from Barcelona in the locker-room before practice. Each player would know his responsibility.

This initiative proved successful in introducing a new tactical shape, teaching individual roles, helping team members appreciate others' roles and understanding how one action stimulates a chain of responses. The excitement and novelty of the approach led players to adopt the unself-ish team mindset necessary to make the tactical shape work effectively. Aptitudes were synchronised, and individual talents and mindsets were co-ordinated into an organised, cohesive team production. The coach achieved his objective. He made this group of young players better than they thought they could be! With this increased team confidence, the coach slowly began to move the team away from the Barcelona concept to develop their own team personality.

Moving in Harmony

A major change in soccer tactics has occurred in recent years. The lesson of major championships, especially in Europe, is that success lies in having a number of attacking players who can operate at high speed under intense pressure and in increasingly smaller spaces. Even the technical demands on back players are increasing, as is the need for goalkeepers to be able to transform defence swiftly into attack. Top clubs like Bayern Munich and Barcelona have led the way in releasing players from a rigid tactical formation. Players like Robben and Messi are free to break into any area of the field where they see productive space. The emphasis of play is now on speed, surprise, fluidity and interchangeability.

However, the key to tactical success remains the same—11 players moving in harmony in defence, in transition and in attack. So although coaches aim to make their players' movement more flexible and creative, they must also coach the adjustment of those players not directly involved to retain the overall cohesion and harmony of the team.

The German National Team demonstrated the power of a team in harmony when winning the 2014 World Cup in Brazil. Miroslav Klose, who became the World Cup's all-time record goal scorer, described his team's efficient and stylish performance as 'super-blend': 'We are a unit, we super-blend in training and it shows on the pitch' (Wilson 2014a, p S6).

A challenge of modern coaching is to create that disciplined mindset of freedom and adjustment, to synch the varied abilities of 11 players into an effective whole—a superblend!

Building Team Cohesion

In games decided on defining moments, the team with greater cohesion is more likely to take advantage of the opportunities. For coaches, building team co-ordination is both a science, through defining and teaching integrated strategies that allow players complementary roles, and an art, by having the personality and persuasive powers to get the whole squad of individual players to commit to the plan and share a common goal.

At every club, certainly at the professional level, the challenge is to get strong-minded individual players from a variety of backgrounds to function with a collective mindset and as a cohesive unit through each long and difficult season.

Players in general are motivated to play

- for themselves to gain personal benefits and fulfilment,
- for significant others,
- for the coach to earn admiration and loyalty,
- for teammates out of friendship and respect and
- for club and country to achieve status.

The challenge of soccer demands that players become strong characters and that coaches be sensitive to their personal agendas. But teams win only when they are cohesive (**T**ogether **E**verybody **A**chieves **M**ore); therefore, players must accept the importance of the team agenda. Players must be willing to move from 'me' to 'we', although smart coaches always try to satisfy both team and individual needs.

This process is not easy, and a level of tension will always be present within teams. Every coach has problems inspiring players to overcome their preconceptions about each other and overcome their doubts about themselves.

Because building and maintaining team co-ordination is a dynamic process, my role, especially with teams threatened by repeated disruption, includes conducting continual mental health checks.

The checklist includes these questions:

- What are the signs that indicate co-ordination?
- What are the signs that indicate dysfunction?
- What are the immediate hot spots that need to be dealt with?

Observe and Learn

When Steve McClaren became head coach of FC Twente in Holland, he asked the existing staff whether they had any plans prepared for preseason. His excellent assistant coach, Erik Ten Hag, produced a well-thought-out, detailed, day-by-day programme. Steve therefore had the unexpected advantage of being able to stand back, observe and check his new team for a six-week period.

- What does each player do well, how, when and where?
- What type of game feels natural to the team?
- What combination of players works well?
- What is the personality of the team?
- What kind of coaching do they respond best to?

This period gave Steve clues about how to synch the various aptitudes of his squad of talented players into a cohesive team unit, one that went on to win the Dutch Eredivisie for the first time.

Developing Awareness

The synchronization of individual player aptitudes into co-ordinated team play depends on the development of awareness. From the age of 10, players have to learn to look beyond themselves and the ball and see the big picture of their position on the field in relation to their teammates and the opposition.

Learning to make order out of chaos is not easy at any level of competitive team sport. I witness this first hand even in international teams. With players assembled from different clubs, frequent changes caused by injury and shortage of practice time, coaches struggle to recreate the cohesion and fluidity that their selected players show on a weekly basis with their club teams. It is no wonder that coaches with limited preparation time with international or other representative sides focus on set pieces such as free kicks or corners, where they have great control and can ensure a high level of player awareness.

Awareness is the ability of the player to scan the ever-changing situation in the playing environment, anticipate future conditions and make and implement correct decisions. Soccer is a game of read (seeing and recognizing the emerging pattern of play) and react (producing the right physical, technical and tactical responses). As soccer becomes a quicker and more sophisticated game tactically, the ability of players to read and react will be increasingly valued.

Reading the game involves several elements:

- Experience and tactical knowledge—game-playing intelligence
- Ability to see or hear all the information available
- Clear communication (signals or calls) with teammates
- Ability to reject irrelevant information
- Evaluation of the state of the game—making the right decisions for the moment
- Use of preknowledge—information on the opposition and preparation leading up to the game

Reacting swiftly and successfully is influenced by the following:

- Technique—good technique equals freedom
- Conditions—playing surface, weather
- Fatigue
- Emotional state—ability to recover from errors
- Playing in an unfamiliar position or shape
- Playing with new or unfamiliar team members

Learning to read and react is developed by playing small-sided games. Whereas the big picture of 11 versus 11 can confuse and defeat younger players, small-sided games offer an ideal progression by breaking the big picture into smaller pieces. Players have more chance to be successful in the time available, thus breeding confidence. Besides being more involved in the game, players learn more quickly by having a constant stream of read-and-react scenarios to deal with, simplified to ensure greater success. Most important, a greater understanding of team co-ordination and better awareness develops.

Coaches teach their players to read and react successfully in four key stages.

1. Perfecting Techniques

Objectives:

- Acquire necessary basic techniques
- Begin to co-ordinate player movements with those of teammates

Method used:

- Repetition of technique in fixed or variable practice conditions without active opponents

2. Techniques, Choice and Skill

Objectives:

- Develop observation, anticipation and decision making in response to choice of action
- Check technical habits under increasing pressure

Methods used:

- Practice drills that build up choice (the range of options available)
- Observations and film analysis

3. Complex Game Skills

Objectives:

- Select the right information, make the correct decisions and implement successful techniques in game situations
- Build up knowledge and experience (memories)

Methods used:

- Small-sided and full games under a variety of challenging conditions
- Film analysis

4. Success in Competition

Objective:

- Achieve optimum technical and tactical performance from each player under maximum physical and psychological stress

Methods used:

- Competition at own level
- Competition at higher levels
- Coach feedback and film analysis

Co-Ordinating Aptitudes

A successful team are a blend and balance of a range of differing personalities, mentalities and aptitudes. Success in modern soccer requires an intricate choreography of many players in a variety of situations. Coaches have to co-ordinate these individual talents into a cohesive, co-ordinated team that can

- deal with a number of tactical shapes,
- be able to change the shape within a game,
- cope with increasing fluidity within individual roles and responsibilities and
- embrace the need for greater tactical awareness and intelligence.

Co-ordinating individual talents into a cohesive yet flexible and fluid system can be difficult and frustrating for the coach. Add to this the requirements of a long season, injuries and squad rotation and the exercise becomes a demanding one that is highly dependent on the players' willingness to be coached and play their defined team roles.

Commitment to what is best for the team leads to cohesion and success. On the great teams you often cannot tell who the best players are. Successful team production depends on

- the right player having the right job,
- the player's belief in the job set,
- the player's feeling of being needed to do the job,
- the player believing that the rest of the team are cheering him or her on and
- each player's acceptance that others are also in the right roles and tactical positions.

Only when coaches deal with these issues will they win the full commitment of individual players to integrate into the team.

Alex Gibson, when he was U18 coach at Manchester City FC, coached his players to do whatever it took to make the team successful. The players were urged to contribute and play a part in a total team effort. Alex was also aware when players were out of synch with the rest of the team and the effect it could have on team cohesion. To deal with this circumstance, Alex shared his concern with the players involved. If that approach did not work, he would involve the whole team. Usually, the peer pressure exerted would bring the player back into a team mindset.

Building Team Co-Ordination

Synchronised aptitudes do not happen by chance. Good coaches create effective and efficient co-ordination in their team-play by building their teams to achieve that purpose.

1. Select Tactics
Each coach has to decide on a way to play that is suitable to the team's age, level and gender. Many coaches make the mistake of trying to adopt tactics that are way beyond the physical, technical or mental abilities of their players. The golden rule is to keep it simple, ensure that the players feel comfortable, work to create some early success and then build from there.

Player Code of Conduct

Put the team first.
Be open towards others.
Respect the opinions of others.
Remember that we are all different.
Treat one another with dignity.
Encourage each other.
Be accountable for your actions.
Be helpful towards others.
Be grateful for help from others.
Be dependable.
Always think positively.

2. Recruit for Specific Roles
Each tactical shape comes with positional roles and responsibilities. Players have to be comfortable in their own roles before they can successfully co-ordinate with other team members. Ill-considered recruitment is likely to be a threat to existing players, particularly when the new players are in similar team positions and roles. Team harmony can suffer. A major mistake in recruiting is to select the most talented players and then finding that their skill set does not fit into any positional role in the team shape. The second biggest mistake is recruiting a player who does not play the position as well as an existing player does!

3. Build In Versatility
Team effectiveness during a long season can be enhanced if some players can play more than one position. The academy of AFC Ajax in Holland coached players in three related positions, such as left back, left midfield and left wing, from the age of 8 to 12. Allowing young players the flexibility to sample different team roles should lead to greater understanding of roles and greater success in interchanging positions.

4. Coach Teams Within Teams
By breaking down the teaching of overall team co-ordination into three units—defence, offense and goalkeeping—coaches can accelerate the development of player understanding of their roles and those of the players alongside them. Coaches then need to ensure that these specialist units do not get detached from the vital overall co-ordination of the

whole team in offense, defence and transition. Coaches must carefully balance the amount of unit teaching to whole-team teaching.

Synching Aptitudes on Offense

The most challenging aspect of team play for a coach is to develop choreographed co-ordination in attacking play. Many of the soccer coaches I come across are former defenders. They are comfortable coaching the defending third of the field, manage in the middle third but are least effective in the attacking third. Attacking play is unpredictable. Players need a great deal of freedom to make decisions on the move. This characteristic poses a real challenge to the aim of getting players to work and move together both on and off the ball.

A helpful coach gives players a framework in which to operate. I discussed this recently with a young coach who was given the role of building effective attacking play. We came up with the following plan for a fully dimensional, multiphased attacking system that provides these elements:

- A simple core setup
- Flexibility to attack in a variety of ways and speeds
- Ability to see an advantage and take it (e.g., overloads)
- Sustainable, multiphased attacks that maintain pressure on defenders

Players must learn to work together in practice so that they can work together in competition.

Photo courtesy of FC Twente.

- Switching between attacking at speed and attacking with much slower deliberation
- Recognising the opponent's strengths and weaknesses
- Clearly defined objectives and production targets that allow, for example,
    - positive entries into the attacking third of the field,
    - crosses into the penalty area, and
    - shots on target.

Having established a framework with which the coach felt comfortable, we then discussed the teaching progression that would help achieve attacking co-ordination:

- Isolate the relevant skills (e.g., crossing the ball, playing wall passes).
- Teach and repeat to develop good habits.
- Increase realism by reducing time and introducing opposition.
- Develop a small-sided games approach.
- Introduce players to the full game.
- Have team meetings to build conceptual knowledge and understand the big picture.
- Support by using film analysis to watch scenarios unfold.
- Encourage innovation and allow positive mistakes (i.e., trying to do the right thing).

The coach followed this programme and is building an effective attacking dimension to his team's play.

Perfecting Seamless Execution

The intelligence of the great coaches is bringing order to chaos and in making a potentially complex game quite simple for their players. Excellence in coaching, like playing, is a case of doing simple things well.

This notion is never tested more than when synching the aptitudes of 11 players (and more on the bench) into a co-ordinated whole. Simplicity is the key. When coaching discussion became too sophisticated at Middlesbrough FC, our senior coach Steve Harrison would bring everybody back to reality by asking, 'Who does what, why, when, how and where?' He would point to the poster on the wall that read:

Simplicity	Repetition
Clarity	Execution

And when selection became confused, Steve would advise, 'Make sure you put round pegs in round holes and square pegs in square holes'.

Brian Clough, the legendary manager of Nottingham Forest, won a European Championship on a simple but powerful philosophy: 'Goal-keepers save, centre-backs head, full-backs tackle, midfielders pass, wingers cross, and strikers score'.

Soccer is a game of reality and illusion. The illusion is that teams win for any number of reasons— previous results, being at home, reputation, tradition and history, media speculation and so on. Reality is that soccer games can be won only by players doing their jobs well—playing hard and with discipline, taking care of the ball and co-ordinating their efforts into an effective team performance. I like the way Steve Mariucci (Gibson, Pratt, Roberts, and Weynes 2001, p 99), former coach of San Francisco 49ers, sums up seamless execution and winning:

> We're not going to win tomorrow because we're much better than them or because we're at home and we're the good guys. Those aren't the reasons we're going to win the football game. That stuff doesn't mean anything, doesn't mean anything. We play harder than them, we play more disciplined than them, we execute our game plan better than they execute their game plan. We take care of the ball better than they take care of the ball. That's why we're going to win the game. You've got to play to that plan.

This important message should be repeated continually in some form: 'We win because we do simple things well and better than our opponents'.

For teams to produce seamless execution, they must have a harmony of physical, technical, tactical, mental and emotional preparation. Such teams will be composed of players willing to learn and adjust their skills to meet the differing functional needs of their team and with a positive, focused and strong mindset.

In championship-winning teams, Real Madrid, for example, player aptitudes are synched in harmony, helping to mould a winning team mindset that creates

- a cohesive organised blend and balance of talents,
- a cohesive organised blend and balance of personalities,
- the satisfying of personal agendas in which each player is able to perform at his or her best,
- a willingness to accept and work with the differing strengths and weaknesses of others and
- the discipline to play a team role that may limit personal opportunities.

Together, these elements create the opportunity for seamless execution. Achieving it is the ultimate challenge for the modern coach.

OVERCOMING UNDERPERFORMANCE AND BUILDING TEAM CO-ORDINATION

Coach Phil had a particular issue undermining his attempts to synch the aptitudes of his team into a co-ordinated system of play—the presence of several under-performers who were adversely affecting team-play. I advised him not to rush into judgement without understanding why these players were not performing to their potential. We discussed several possible causes of underperformance:

- Trouble at home
- Loss of motivation
- Lack of competency
- Lack of knowledge and understanding
- Insecurity.

To turn this small group around, we agreed to do the following:

- Help each player reconnect to the reasons they played soccer.
- Identify and agree with them the key performance issues that were of concern.
- Discuss the likely causes of their performance issues.
- Set up a meeting to communicate our support.
- Remind them of our confidence in them.
- Identify any obstacles outside the players' control.
- Discuss ideas for improvement.
- Agree on action that could be taken.
- Set a date to review progress.

Coach Phil was brilliant. He quickly helped the players find renewed meaning in their soccer. He gave technical advice, acted as a catalyst, involved the help of specialists when needed and played the role of a cheerleader by constantly being positive and encouraging. He did not demand quick results but understood that change would come with systematic, focused repetition and frequent gentle reminders.

Phil was successful in raising the performance levels (and overall team co-ordi-nation) of all but one of the underperformers. That player resisted all efforts. The coach decided that he was incompatible with the team goals, and he was gone!

CHAPTER 9

MANAGING MOOD

Middlesbrough FC was in a slump that was reflected in the mood of the locker-room. Then we recruited Benito Carbone on loan. The tiny Italian arrived on his first day in a powerful Ferrari. Immaculately dressed, Benito collected his kit and flung open the doors of the locker-room announcing, 'Boys, I am here. All is well!'

The assembled players roared with laughter and clapped Benito into the room. Instantly, optimism, confidence and energy seemed to return, and the mood of the team moved from negative to positive. The practice that followed was the best of the season, and three days later the team, inspired by Benito, beat Manchester United 1-0 at Old Trafford.

Understanding the Importance of Team Mood

The mood of a team is reflected in the prevailing emotion shared by the players in the locker-room. This mood state is clear evidence of how the players are defining their present team situation. It can range from positive, optimistic, confident and assertive to negative, pessimistic, anxious and passive. A few influential players are likely to shape the overall mood; emotions are contagious. The actions of Benito Carbone could have been perceived as arrogant, but in a locker-room in the middle of a slump, his optimism and positivity fired the players into a more positive mood state. The collective mood of the locker-room is important because it acts as the catalyst for the team's energy state. For that reason, an assistant coach should learn to judge the mood (and thus the energy state) of the team as they gather at the start of the day and feed the signals to the head coach so that he or she can respond with an appropriate programme of activity for the day ahead.

Experienced coaches understand the importance of managing the everyday mood of the team and can recognise when events and circumstances might cause a change. I constantly advise soccer coaches to study the great coaches of all sports. Former NFL coach Bill Walsh (Walsh, Billick and Peterson 1998, p 340) is especially good on describing the importance of swift responses to changing circumstances to maintain a proactive team mood:

> The career of a head coach can be viewed as a mosaic. It's not a by-product of any one event; rather, it's a consequence of a whole series of events. Some of these events occur simply as a factor of the passage of time. Others evolve as circumstances and situations change.
>
> How well the coach anticipates and handles these events can affect the performance and general well-being of the team. Dealt with properly, these occurrences can serve a productive purpose in the learning process. On the other hand, if these incidents are handled in an inadequate manner, they can become pitfalls on the road to success.
>
> Accordingly, one of the greatest challenges facing the head coach is the need to be able to react appropriately to changing circumstances. In other words, regardless of the situation, you must be able to make a well-considered decision.

Walsh is describing a skill that coaches can really acquire only through experience. In my mentoring of head coaches I describe this as the process of building up a pack of cards as the coach's career progresses. Each card is a possible response to a situation that may occur. Mood-threatening incidents happen to all teams, but the great coaches usually have at least one card up their sleeve ready to resolve the situation.

The constant battle between positive and negative team mood in the season (and the higher the level and challenge of competition are, the more the team mood can be threatened at any moment) is recognised by Dr Rosabeth Moss Kanter (2002, p 45), a Harvard business professor who understands sport:

> Good moods are both causes and effects. Winning puts people in a good mood and being in a good mood makes it easier to win. The contagion of positive emotions can help improve co-operation, decrease conflict and underscore more positive perceptions of everyone's task performance. Negative emotions have the reverse effect.
>
> Moods are catching, especially among people who know they depend on one another.
>
> Moods spread from person to person in surprisingly subtle ways.

Nurturing a Winning Mood at
FC Barcelona

Report on a visit by Tom Bates, performance coach, West Bromwich Albion FC Academy:

1. **Uphold the culture**. Upon arrival, every member of staff is greeted by the president with the message, 'The main priority of your position is to uphold the spirit and culture of the club because this will last long after we are gone'.

2. **Respect in action**. Before practice every player greets the families of the other players. Every player helps move equipment. Before every match the opposition are honoured with team applause.

3. **Staying positive**. Coaches trust players to play. Coaches communicate no destructive criticism, no stressful reactions and no negative input. Performance is as important as outcome.

4. **Setting standards**. The day after a big game the first team trains hard for 45 minutes. The coach explains, 'We believe the body follows what the mind tells it to do. It's our way'.

5. **Humility and togetherness**. The president eats in the public dining area, and anyone can sit with him. All lunch tables are shared between all teams, and everyone is encouraged to be together and interact.

6. **Labour of love**. Every member of staff is reminded by the president, 'My job and your job is a labour of love, and if it is not we will fail'.

7. **First the person, then the player**. The education programme is regarded as highly as soccer development, creating well-rounded, thinking players with wisdom. Fifteen senior players are studying for degrees alongside their soccer career.

8. **The football family**. One of the players, Eric Abidal, was fighting cancer. The club instructed a film to be made of the way Eric contributed to the club in his tackling, running and meeting the competitive challenge. All people at the club watched the film to remind them of their connection to each other.

Coaching successfully, therefore, requires the understanding of a team's emotional state and the ability to build and retain a good, positive, collective team mood throughout the season. From 2003 through to 2013 Everton FC consistently achieved beyond their talent base under the leadership of then manager David Moyes. David created a winning team mood in several ways:

- Setting realistic objectives
  - Finishing in league position of fourth through eighth
  - Making a good cup run
  - Finishing ahead of Liverpool FC (local rivals!)
- Driving production himself
  - Setting high standards
  - Encouraging teaching and learning
  - Demanding work ethic every day
- Building healthy relationships
  - Caring for the players
  - Appointing personable support staff
  - Selecting an inspirational captain (Phil Neville)

To visit Everton was to see a motivational climate in action. The day had purpose and organisation, energy and activity, communication and humour. The infectious mood demonstrated the power of a club where players enjoy coming to work, even after a defeat.

In a highly competitive league, team mood is threatened continually. The then assistant manager at Everton, Steve Round, confirmed, 'The hardest thing each week remains shaping the mood of the team so that they are triggered to play on the Saturday game day'.

© Gary Houlder/Lithium/age fotostock

Addressing players in the locker-room can be a key moment in influencing mood and momentum.

Humour Releases Tension

Playing Steaua Bucharest away from home was a tough challenge, especially for the four young (17- and 18-year-old) players in the Middlesbrough FC team. Despite the depressing physical appearance of the locker-room, all was well until an armed police officer announced that the game would be delayed for about 20 minutes. I watched the mood of the team change as the rhythm of preparation was broken. As I wondered how to change the mood back, Coach Steve Harrison took over. Steve, a great coach of defence and a very funny man, began a series of silly walks imitating certain players and staff. When the official came to summon us to the field, the team were laughing and the positive mood had been restored. The young players did well. The team lost 0-1, but the result put us in a good position to win the return leg!

At any stage of the season a coach and his or her team can be leading the pack, on an extended winning streak, just holding position, on an extended losing streak, in a slump or suffering from a thunderbolt, an unexpected setback.

Any of these situations has an enormous effect on team mindset and the way that the players feel. How the coach manages the collective feelings of the team (their mood) greatly influences his or her ability to control performance.

Teams operate with momentum; they are either gaining positive momentum or accumulating negative momentum. Failure and success are not single events but part of the pathway of the team. Many things are carried over from game to game, and they help shape the mood of the locker-room and have a direct effect on team performance on the field. Every performance is shaped by the previous one unless something changes the mood, therefore affecting momentum. From time to time extremely strong negatives cannot immediately be counterbalanced by a single positive act; for instance, Sir Alex Ferguson's retirement has had a lingering effect on Manchester United. Patience is needed in transition. Enough positives must be built up to create a tipping point away from negative momentum.

Several key reminders are useful for coaches:

- Understand what represents a positive team mood for your team.
- Develop a range of strategies that encourage this mood.
- Appreciate that you and your staff are models of such a mood.
- Balance the need for performance challenge with the need for relationship support.
- Recruit for positive character (mood consistency) as well as talent.
- Be aware of factors that may threaten team mood.
- Act quickly to defeat potential negatives.

- Develop strategies that take the team from negative mood back to positive mood.
- Value the use of humour in releasing tension.
- Never take a positive team mood for granted.
- Build continuity and stability—avoid making change for change's sake.

Keeping Team Mood Positive

Soccer is a succession of challenges. When the mood of the team is good, and they face each situation positively, with confidence and energy, they are more likely to achieve on the field. If they fail to meet those challenges, their mood state will likely change towards negative and make the next challenge more difficult to overcome. Mood and subsequent performance are clearly related (see figure 9.1). Coaches must know at all times where their team are on the continuum so that they can take appropriate action.

Recognising Mood Change

Every team will experience highs and lows through the season. The trick is to get neither too high (to become complacent) nor too low (to become overanxious). One of the problems that coaches face is that they don't recognise the mood changes until too late (see table 9.1).

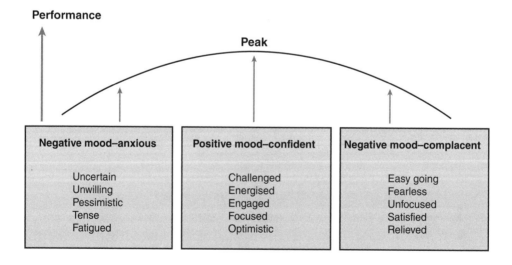

FIGURE 9.1 Mood state and performance.

TABLE 9.1 **Signs Indicating a Change of Team Mood From Positive to Negative State**

Increase in	Decrease in
Anxiety, depression	Enthusiasm, energy
Sickness, minor injuries	Communication, eye contact
Tension, conflict	Enjoyment, humour
Indiscipline	Work ethic, responsibility
Blaming, excuses	Confidence, belief
Pessimism, negative self-talk	Teamship, co-operation
Mistakes, mediocrity	Learning, quality
Hiding under pressure	Focus, attention
Accepting defeat easily	Emotional control
Off-the-field issues	Voluntary extra work

They are either too close to the team to see or are overpowered by their own emotions and agenda and ignore the players' feelings. I often find that coaches are the last to recognise that their team are sliding into a negative mood state. Helping coaches regain the big picture is often a valuable contribution of the coach mentor, visiting sport psychologist or even a concerned parent.

Maintaining Stability and Continuity

Stability is key to success, according to a study by the Professional Football Players Observatory (PFPO), a FIFA-backed research group. This study of 13,000 players across Europe provided the profile of the average

Controlling Mood Determines a World Cup Final

In 2010 the England Women's National Team reached the rugby World Cup Final to be held in the Stoop Stadium, London. I have never seen a team in such a positive mood state as it travelled to the stadium. But the expected crowd of 6,000 turned out to be 14,000, and the team bus had to stop 300 metres from the locker-rooms. The team had to make an unexpected walk through the crowd, including families and friends, and when they eventually made the locker-room they were weighed down by the high level of expectation and the consequences of defeat. The mood changed from positive to negative, and the Final was lost!

The lesson was not lost on head coach Gary Street. Before the next World Cup Final in Paris in 2014, Gary was ready. Despite pressure from well-wishers and media, Gary reduced undue intrusion from the sideshow by controlling external influences and keeping England focused on performance. The England team won a decisive victory.

club squad and its relationship to success. It prompted the following response by Jonathan Northcroft (2011) in the *Sunday Times*:

> Money talks, tactics tell, management matters. But one factor appears most important when building successful sides: stability. The longer players stay at a club, the more stable the first team success becomes. Manchester United have the most settled squad in Europe and Barcelona the third in a survey of 534 clubs from 36 Nations.
>
> What's more, compose a Premier League based on stability and it looks uncannily like the actual table. Stability is also a constant of clubs who win the Champions League.

As table 9.2 illustrates, stability and continuity in a team can affect performance positively by restricting the amount of change and distraction and promoting a more sustained positive team mood state. Stability helps protect the mental and emotional security of the players from the three pressures that teams face: (1) tension from within (team chemistry, selection, and so on), (2) the opposition and (3) tension from external factors (media, family and so on).

Retaining a positive mood state and psychological security whilst handling these pressures is vital to all players but especially women players, who often have a greater need to feel emotional security.

The North Carolina women's soccer head coach, Anson Dorrance (Dorrance and Nash 2014), stresses the importance of relationships to reduce tension in women players.

TABLE 9.2   A Typical Manchester United Team in 2011 Showing the Effect of Continuity and Stability

Player	Seasons at the club	Trophies won
Van der Saar	7	5
O'Shea	12	8
Brown	14	11
Smalling	1	0
Giggs	18	20
Nani	4	4
Carrick	5	5
Evra	6	7
Scholes	17	15
Rooney	8	8
Hernandez	1	0

All the female players on the team have to feel like they have a more personal connection with the coach and each of those relationships must be unique. They have to feel you care about them personally or have some kind of connection beyond the game. In a nutshell, they want to experience your humanity.

This objective cannot be achieved without stability and continuity in the players and staff supporting the team.

Too much change, conflict or distraction sets off the following chain reaction:

- Uncertainty.
- Uncertainty leads to distraction and anxiety.
- Anxiety leads to mental and physical tension.
- Too much tension leads to poor performance!

Former Arsenal player Martin Keown (2014, p 66), writing in the *Daily Mail*, analysed why manager David Moyes lost his job at Manchester United and emphasised lack of continuity and stability:

When you start at a new club, you need to work out quickly who your best players are and then formulate a system that will suit them. Moyes failed to do either, picking 51 different starting XIs in his 51 games in charge.

After less than one year David Moyes left Manchester United. The start of the 2014–15 season saw Dutchman Louis van Gaal installed as the new head coach. The stability and continuity during Sir Alex Ferguson's era, as illustrated in table 9.2, had been lost. Overcoming the change will take time, as van Gaal has pointed out.

Interpreting Results

Team mood is significantly affected by game results. A win or a loss significantly affects the mindset and mood of the team, especially when it occurs as part of a winning or losing run. The coach who has built a good team mindset and mood must ensure that game results are interpreted in a way that challenges the team but does not cause untoward damage to the underlying positive state. Nothing demonstrates the emotional intelligence of the coach more than those first few moments of dealing with the team after an unexpected result.

The Power of an Apt Team Talk

In the era of their legendary manager Jim Smith, Derby County FC had gone on a 12-game unbeaten run and then crashed 0-3 away from home to championship rivals Sunderland. The effect in the locker-room after the game was more like a disaster than a defeat. The players sat in total silence, waiting for the wrath of their fierce, straight-talking manager. Jim walked in, sat down and to everyone's surprise said, 'Thank God for that! I don't know about you lot, but I haven't been able to sleep at night with the pressure of this unbeaten run'.

'Tell you what', he continued, 'let's all have a good two days off and then we'll start to build a new run on Tuesday'.

After that speech the Derby players picked themselves up and held their form until the end of the season, earning promotion to the Premier League. That closure after a defeat proved the power of a well-timed team talk from a manager who knew exactly how to judge the mood of the dressing room.

The esteemed psychologist Martin Seligman (1998) describes people in difficult emotional situations as being in a state of either learned optimism or learned helplessness. Coaches who are learned optimists interpret the situation in a positive, healthy, developmental manner. They absorb the emotions of the result, reflect and find perspective and regain balance to use the learning to develop their team. Coaches who lack emotional intelligence descend into learned helplessness because they cannot absorb the emotional effect of the result and thus lose both balance and perspective. This reaction can be damaging in a locker-room where a team has competed for 90 or more minutes and need the coach to tell them how to feel.

Table 9.3 compares the response to defeat of an optimistic coach and a pessimistic coach. Both feel the pain, but the optimistic coach has developed a way of explaining the result in a way that challenges but does not undermine the team mood, morale and progress.

Undoubtedly, coaches who are realistically optimistic generate a more effective and longer lasting positive team mood state. An emotionally intelligent attitude has taught them to deal with, and not react to, setbacks by always

- overcoming their personal pain,
- looking for the good in any situation,
- seeking the valuable lesson in any setback,
- looking for the solutions in every problem and
- seeking perspective by relating to the team's overarching aims.

When compared with this agenda, who would want to play for a pessimist?

TABLE 9.3 **Comparing Optimistic and Pessimistic Coaches When Explaining a Defeat**

Optimistic coach	Pessimistic coach
This is disappointing. It's just a temporary setback. This is just one game—a bad day at the office. I am happy I prepared the team well. I will try harder next time. I can help the team recover.	This is awful. This will last a long time. Defeat undermines everything we do—it's always the same. It's all my fault. I'm useless. I feel like giving up. I feel helpless to affect things.
Message to the team	**Message to the team**
Disappointing, but it's just one game. You can do better. Some good play and effort. Lots to work on. We can learn from this. See you all at practice.	Awful—look at our league position. Long way back. Nobody played well. So much to get right. Let's get out of here.

Changing the Story

The mood state of a team is the story they are telling themselves at any time. This chapter has discussed many potential influences on mood and the fact that it can change quickly from a positive story full of confidence to a negative story dominated by anxiety. When such a change occurs, the coach needs to find a strategy to change the story back to the positive as quickly as possible. Coaches might use any of these strategies:

- A meeting with senior players to identify the problem
- A full team meeting to share ownership of the problem
- A guest inspirational speaker to relight the fire
- A highlights film to remind the team how good they are
- A break from practice to give everybody time to reflect
- A change from practice to swimming, go-karting or some other fun activity
- A revision of team goals to provide new focus
- A change of personnel on the team or staff

Depending on the age, gender and level of the team, a coach must find a suitable (and often speedy) response to a declining mood state. An extreme example (not recommended!) was the action of a professional coach who was upset with his team mood as they had their prematch walk. He decided to shake them up by jumping into the river they were walking by. On this occasion the story changed and the team won.

HOW AN ASSISTANT COACH INFLUENCES TEAM MOOD

Rob is the assistant coach of a professional senior men's team. A passionate soccer man, Rob has learned the value of emotional intelligence and has developed a realistic yet optimistic coaching style. He knows certain truths at the start of every season:

- The team will play a total of 50 to 60 games, 3 every two weeks.
- In a good season the team win 4, tie 2 and lose 4 of every 10 games.
- Team mood is an important factor in season-long performance.
- Team mood will be challenged by a series of highs and lows.
- Team mood will also be challenged by the constant change at the club.

Rob's first step to ensuring a positive team mood is to be the centre for communication. Because the manager is often busy, Rob makes himself available and sets himself the goal of talking to everybody on the squad at least once every day. He also deliberately spends time in the locker-room getting a feel for the prevailing mood. Finally, to ensure that he stays up to date with the team 'story', Rob has a weekly clear-the-air meeting with the captain and three trusted seniors.

Rob also works hard to act as a model for a good mood state. Always in early and looking good, Rob spreads passion, enthusiasm and energy to the players arriving. A real locker-room coach, Rob often quotes John Wooden to his players: 'Make today your masterpiece'.

Whatever the context, Rob tries hard to make his club a good and enjoyable place to work. He understands that players need challenges every day but also that hard work can be fun. Always sincere and purposeful in his teaching, Rob knows when the mood of the team is down. At those times he injects a fun game to raise energy levels.

His job as assistant coach allows Rob the chance to stay on the pulse of the team and give the manager early warnings of potential mood swings. He knows that his manager values his assistant's suggestions on how to change the story. Rob understands that critical incidents are inevitable under pressure and fatigue but believes in early recognition, firm but sensitive corrective action and moving on quickly. Rob tries hard to be at his best in the locker-room after games. When the manager and the team are threatened with loss of emotional control, Rob becomes the focal point for composure, positivity and optimism. The fact that his team are recognised as upbeat and enthusiastic throughout the season is great credit to this young assistant coach.

Part III

PERFORMANCE

A winning mindset overcomes barriers to performance and drives teams towards sustainable excellence.

Chapter 10

COMPETING COHESIVELY

Key defining moments for coaches who are building a winning team mindset is how they deal with goals scored or conceded by their team. The latter especially is a major test of team mindset. Responses can be divisive or blaming, 'It was your fault,' or a collective acceptance of responsibility, 'We all could have done better'. Coaches must not let a moment of high emotion divide a collective team mindset in a negative way.

The best way to treat a goal scored or a goal conceded is to consider it the responsibility of the whole team. A great coach shows the film of the goal scored, enjoys the moment with the team and then works backwards: 'Let's see who made the assist. Now let's see who got the ball to him. Now let's see who won the ball back for us to begin the play.' Celebrating every aspect of the offense builds a cohesive team dynamic. Similarly, the goal conceded is not simply the fault of the goalkeeper. It can usually be tracked back to show four or five players who could have defended better and therefore share responsibility. Accepting individual and collective responsibility is the underlying discipline that leads to effective team cohesion and winning games.

Coaching Team Cohesion

The reason that identifying the best player on a great team is difficult is that every player makes significant contributions. With a team-first achievement culture, every player strives to set up teammates for success. The great coaches never miss an opportunity to point out how winning derives from total team effort, and they constantly preach collective performance. They instinctively know (and have confirmed through experience) that co-ordination and cohesion are the keys to team victory despite there being no statistics for best chemistry or unselfishness and so on.

As the 2014 World Cup winners, Germany demonstrated the power of togetherness. Their team concept was singled out as a major factor in their success. Captain Philipp Lahm in the *Daily Telegraph* (Wilson 2014b, p S5) hailed Germany's triumph of collective brilliance over individual talents: 'It's unbelievable what we have achieved. Whether we have the best individual players doesn't matter at all, you just need to have the best team'.

Geoff Colvin (2008, p 137) in his book *Talent Is Overrated* also recognises that a team's performance is not determined simply by the individual abilities of their players:

> Applying the principles of great performance to team development is not conceptually difficult. The same basic elements that work for individuals—well-designed practice activities, coaching, repetition, feedback, self-regulation, building knowledge, and mental models—all work for teams as well. The problems are practical. They centre on forces within the team that prevent it from realising the benefits of the great performance approach.

Colvin goes on to describe such negative forces, including picking the wrong team members, competing agendas, unresolved conflicts and unwillingness to face the real issues.

Teams can transcend their talent level with coached cohesion and chemistry, but they can fall short of their potential when division and strife are present between team members. The further that soccer teams progress and advance (thus the greater the rewards), then the more coaches have to counteract selfishness. Coaches teach that the team come first, but the real test is safeguarding the team against talented but selfish and divisive players. Tolerating individual selfishness has destroyed many good teams!

The history of Manchester United is littered with great players suddenly leaving when Sir Alex Ferguson insisted that they could not be allowed to become bigger than the club. Certainly, no player at a club is irrelevant. All players should be respected and included, but no individual is indispensable.

One of the thresholds of developing from a good coach to a great coach occurs when the coach starts to select the best 11, not the 11 best. This coach has realised that winning goes beyond physical skills and that a positive team mindset, in which players willingly co-operate and play as a co-ordinated unit, elevates the team to the point where the whole becomes more than the sum of the parts, thus demonstrating the synergy of a cohesive team.

Here are key questions for the coach to answer.

- What unites your team?
- What are your common purposes?

- What actions bring your team together?
- What words represent your core team values?

Team Cohesion Starts With Mindset

Although team cohesion is seen in action as a physical, technical and tactical co-ordination of effort, it begins with mental and emotional decisions. Each player chooses to suspend self-interest for the sake of the team. This movement from 'me' thinking to 'we' thinking signals the start of team building and cohesive performance.

When Chelsea lost to Atletico Madrid in the semi-final of the Champions League, Jose Mourinho, the Chelsea manager, pointed out a 'me' thinking problem that prevented wide player Eden Hazard from helping his fullback when the team conceded the vital first goal:

> Jose Mourinho has accused his star player, Eden Hazard, of being unable to sacrifice himself fully for the team and bluntly told the Belgium winger that he was to blame for the crucial first goal . . . . [Mourinho said,] 'It's normal because he's not the kind of player ready to sacrifice himself 100 per cent for the team and his mates. Eden is the kind of player who is not so mentally ready to look back at his left-back and live his life for him'. (Wilson 2014c, p S2)

Encouraging players to move from a 'me' mindset to a more collective 'we' mindset depends on trust. Coaches must demonstrate trust in the player by saying, 'I believe in you', and win the player's trust in the coaching process by saying something like, 'Everything done is for the good of the team'. Trust between players must also build, as coaches continually encourage them to rely on each other in practice and games.

Any team game is based on a mental and emotional commitment to togetherness, in good times and bad. Trust is the emotional glue that holds a team together. Teams that fail are plagued by a lack of trust where the prevailing emotion is one of fear—fear of failure, fear of the coaches, fear of what others think about them.

All coaches, at whatever level their teams play, have to work continuously to combat fears that sow the seeds for a loss of trust and can arise at any point. Coaches must be especially aware of situations that can suddenly threaten the collective team mindset, togetherness and

Sign on Locker-Room Wall

Great teams demand and expect a lot out of one another.
Your teammates expect it out of you
And you from them.
When it gets to this, the sky is the limit!

cohesion. These potential conflict situations can threaten team cohesiveness at any time:

- Change in the team
- Change of tactics
- Conflict over task or social roles
- Poor communication
- Introducing a new player or coach
- Departure of a key player
- Injury to a key player
- Unexpected defeat
- Personality clash
- Failing team captaincy or leadership
- Power struggle for team leadership

Coaches need to act quickly to defuse negative emotions and find ways to emphasise that the positive forces that hold the team together are more significant than any divisive situations likely to pull the team apart.

Maintaining Harmony

Winning is a collective effort. Before games, coaches must ask the following questions:

- Are we physically ready?
- Are we tactically ready?

'Heavy Shirt'

The introduction of Wayne Rooney, a superbly talented but precocious young man who carried a problem player label, into the Manchester United dressing room could have brought all sorts of team cohesion problems. However, several factors minimised the issue.

- Wayne found a cause bigger than himself.
- The squad had excellent stability.
- The team had a core of strong players and personalities.
- The squad would make Wayne a better player.
- Roy Keane was a formidable captain.
- The team were already good.

Wearing the 'heavy shirt' of high expectations, Wayne quickly conformed to established team norms and continues to contribute to United's continued success.

- Are we mentally ready?
- So, are we together as a team?

Team cohesion, a team in tune with their individual and collective responsibilities, is based on two critical factors.

1. Mental clarity—every player knowing clearly what is expected of him or her and all teammates in every possible game situation
2. Trust—the faith and belief that every player will do his or her job correctly, especially under pressure

Soccer is a complex game of physical chess that demands a high number of interactions (at speed and under fatigue) from players all over the field. This requirement has increased as teams have adopted changes in style, such as FC Barcelona's high passing and positional interchange play, thus demanding greater attention to team co-ordination. Equally, team cohesiveness is tested by a player management strategy like Manchester United's successful squad rotation under Sir Alex Ferguson.

Getting all players into a positive team mindset that gets and keeps them on the same page within the boundaries of agreed team-first behaviours is an important aspect of the coaching role. Both internal factors, such as nonselection, injury and conflict, and external stresses, such as media, fans, agents and parents, can force players either alone or in small groups to position themselves outside the accepted behaviours of the team. Coaches need to remember that whilst they are dealing with an internal lack of harmony, they are not fully focused on preparing to beat the next opponent. For that reason, they need to create an environment that maintains a motivational climate which encourages everybody to co-operate. This keeps as many players inside the team boundaries as possible and leaves a way back for those who may find themselves temporarily on the outside. Thus, coaches must take these actions:

- Determine their non-negotiables—'To play on this team, you must . . .'
- Agree team boundaries with the team by asking, 'What kind of team do we want to be?'
- Establish clear team and individual goals by stating how players will be accountable
- Have a policy of inclusion by not ignoring anyone
- Communicate constantly, remembering to include a great deal of listening
- Remove fear, which is the prevailing emotion on divided teams
- Deal proactively with situations that cause players to step outside team boundaries.

Soccer teams increasingly reflect today's multicultural society, and cultural differences can get in the way of cohesion and teamwork. Lack of understanding and respect for cultural differences can be an underlying cause of conflict and poor performance. Coaches must avoid imposing a monoculture approach. They should pay special attention to their use and style of authority, aiming only for respectful and legitimate control. They need to communicate clearly and do lots of listening to understand differing perceptions. In their decision making, they should seek to increase a feeling of shared ownership with all cultures within the team.

Maintaining Inclusion Within a Squad

A constant strain on cohesion is the difficulty of managing a squad of players whilst depending on the few more talented players to win games. Generally, any squad divide into three groups:

- Starters (players who feel successful)
- Back-up players who are regularly used (players with generally neutral feelings)
- Back-up players who are rarely used (players who may feel frustrated)

The culture and psychological stability of the squad depends on the relative proportions of these three groups. Coaches must ensure that as many players as possible have a significant stake in the team's success by keeping the size of the squad manageable, ensuring that all players clearly understand their role in the overall plan, acknowledging and appreciating everybody's contribution and treating players (and staff) well so that no one wants to leave the club.

One potential disruption faced every game day is the possible negative behaviour of the players on the bench or not selected. When this group do not feel part of the team, their attitude and commitment decreases whilst their subversive complaining can increase. Because victims always try to recruit others to their cause, the psychological stability of the team can be threatened. Coaches must help these minor-role players connect to the team by stressing their importance to the team in front of the team, acknowledging them publicly, involving them as much as possible and finding ways to keep them integrated.

Tying Team Cohesion and Performance Together

The best way to understand the effect of team cohesion on performance is to study high-performing teams in action. A great example over the past few years has been the FC Barcelona team built by former coach Pep Guardiola. The first thing noticeable is their passion to achieve, their willingness to work hard and their toughness in persisting through the whole game. Individuals, great players in their own right, sacrifice themselves to the needs and discipline of their roles within the team. Their play shows a sense of calm purpose, and players recover well from the occasional setback. A closer look at Barcelona also reveals a happy team that have good morale and strong interpersonal relationships.

All coaches must work to establish a level of cohesion that builds a climate for team success. Figure 10.1 shows that when a coach works on team cohesion, a greater level of individual satisfaction emerges. This satisfaction should be based on both task cohesion, a clear picture of roles and responsibilities, and social cohesion, a feeling of inclusion and appreciation as part of the team. This feel-good factor leads to increased optimism, energy and application to the task of winning together. The inevitable result is improved performances and more wins, which in turn reward and strengthen team cohesion. At any level winning games is the most powerful cohesive force.

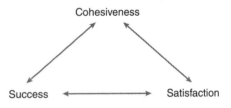

FIGURE 10.1   The cohesion cycle.

To coach others, coaches themselves must be in a good place mentally and remember that their mental stability and emotional control have highly public consequences. Whatever the coach is feeling, she or he must be sure that negatives are not, directly or indirectly, transmitted to players or supporters. One of the greatest qualities of outstanding coaches is their ability to hold their nerve and remain composed.

Nothing will destroy team cohesion and performance faster than a coach who creates instability, constant change and uncertainty and who lacks emotional intelligence by constantly undermining relationships.

Coaches can help their personal psychological stability by

- defining their coaching objectives and purpose clearly and realistically,
- having a clear plan and sticking to it,

- being optimistic rather than pessimistic,
- emphasising performance as well as outcome,
- sharing ownership of the team's development with players and staff,
- treating mistakes as learning opportunities and
- dealing with setbacks and not reacting emotionally to them.

Seven Steps to Team Cohesion

The following seven stages (see figure 10.2) outline the coaching process that aims to build and maintain strong team cohesion.

1. Strong Trustworthy Leadership From the Coach

Leadership is the starting point because of the effect that the knowledge, experience, and style of the leader can have (positively or negatively) on the team and those who support the team. Business management expert David Maister (2002, p 70) identifies four primary components of trustworthiness that can be related to the coach as team leader:

- Credibility through words—'expert, experienced, trustworthy, admits mistakes'
- Reliability through actions—'clear philosophy, consistent, stable'
- Intimacy through emotions—'empathetic, approachable, supportive, enthusiastic'
- Lack of self-orientation and self-interest through motives—'low ego, team oriented, caring, shares credit'

USA National Team soccer player DeMarcus Beasley recognises his coach, Jürgen Klinsmann, as such a leader:

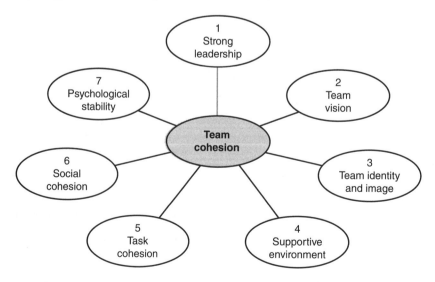

FIGURE 10.2   The steps to team cohesion.

He understands the players' needs. He's a guy who is very enthusiastic about the game still. I know he wishes he probably can still play. He has given us his wisdom. He's very confident when he coaches. We listen because he knows what he's talking about and we can learn a lot from him. (*Championship Performance*, July 2014, Vol 18, Issue 213, p 6)

A coach is seen as a trustworthy leader when acknowledged by the players as high on credibility and reliability and when he or she displays low self-interest. The coach's motives are less to do with him- or herself and more to do with the team's success. As already emphasised in chapter 9, a leader's emotions are contagious, and the mood of the team is often a reflection of the mood of the coach. Therefore, adding intimacy to the equation builds greater trust. An optimistic, enthusiastic and purposeful leader is a powerful unifying force for team cohesion in good times and bad.

The modern player responds better to the coach who is democratic, an expert teacher, supportive and emotionally intelligent. Table 10.1 offers examples of coaches' actions that will build team cohesion through a positive, motivational climate, whereas table 10.2 shows how coaches' actions can destroy team cohesion by creating a demotivating climate.

© MaxiSports | Dreamstime.com

Pep Guardiola is a master of building team cohesion.

TABLE 10.1   Team Cohesion Building

Agree on an exciting goal
Be clear on player roles and responsibilities
Always say 'we', never 'I'
Practise with purpose every day
Stay optimistic but realistic
Keep everybody informed of progress
See setbacks as learning opportunities
Help players appreciate others
Work hard but have fun
Share ideas with the team
Celebrate all successes

TABLE 10.2   Team Resentment Building

Talk about 'my' team, not 'our' team
Be too authoritarian and allow no player ownership
Be poorly organised and offer little explanation
Lack direction and purpose
Set petty rules and conditions
Communicate poorly
Overcoach, resulting in mental fatigue
Overtrain, resulting in physical fatigue
Lack empathy and warmth
Schedule all work and no play
Favour certain players over others

2. Team Vision

For players to commit to the team the coach must present and sell a vision of what the team could achieve—the prize worthwhile! This team vision is an agreement, a covenant that binds the team together, sets the standards and creates the trust and confidence to which a team must fully commit. Table 10.3 illustrates a template for this process, which is meant to be a shared process between coaches and players. A foundation for teamwork is established that binds players together, creates equal footing, helps players understand their responsibilities and prescribes terms for the help and support of teammates.

TABLE 10.3 **Build a Core Covenant for Your Team**

Aim	To win _____
Goals	To _____
	To _____
Values—everyone in our club has these	Respect—our team will _____
	Belief—our team will _____
	Support—our team will _____
	Honesty—our team will _____
	Discipline—our team will _____
	Commitment—our team will _____
	Encouragement—our team will _____
	Enjoyment—our team will_____
Values—what players need from coaches	Feedback—the coaches will _____
	Encouragement—the coaches will _____
	Trust and respect—the coaches will _____
Values—what coaches need from players	Respect—the players will _____
	Focus—the players will _____
	Courtesy—the players will _____
	Honesty—the players will _____
	Timekeeping—the players will _____
	Commitment—the players will _____
	Enthusiasm—the players will _____
Values—that shape behaviour	Readiness—our team will _____
	Focus—our team will _____
	Responsibility—our team will _____
	Determination—our team will _____
	Communication—our team will _____
	Discipline—our team will _____
	Respect—our team will _____
Team message (example)	We keep our heads up at all times.
	We have faith and belief in ourselves and each other.

3. Team Identity and Image

Players are more likely to commit to a team that have a strong identity and a powerful self-image. Just as professional teams understand they have to represent the club brand (think Real Madrid), so youth teams and clubs can brand themselves within their resources to become attractive to the modern generation of players. Elements such as team name, team uniforms, facilities, website, honours boards and so on all reinforce the image of a club that consists of teams worth committing to.

4. Supportive Environment

Strong leadership is about control, teaching and constant challenge, but increasingly it is also about providing support for a generation of players who struggle with authority and responsibility. Players will accept the challenge of responsibility for their team role, but they must also feel that everything is being done to help them be successful. Key support structures that build positive relationships and team cohesion include the following:

- Individual performance reviews with honest feedback and agreed action plans
- Individual teaching time
- A policy of inclusion
- Group meetings to ensure that players are listened to
- Constant communication that keeps every player up to date
- Appreciation of talent and reward for effort
- Celebration of all successes
- Fun and never letting the pressure of playing beat the pleasure of playing

5. Task Cohesion

This process is highly dynamic. Task cohesion can function or fall apart at any moment in the season. It is influenced by its relationship to social cohesion. Figure 10.3*a* illustrates that in a team established for recreational soccer, social cohesion—enjoying the occasion socially—has priority over task cohesion. For a professional team task, illustrated in figure 10.3*b*, working together to win is of far more importance than social cohesion, and in the short term can, if necessary, operate without it. Figure 10.3*c* illustrates a balanced situation in which task and social cohesion are in harmony, and both forces are geared to facilitating success. Whilst happy teams are not necessarily successful and successful teams are not necessarily happy, getting the best out of the modern player will only be achieved in an environment where they are socially relaxed and content, meaning this is a key task of modern coaching.

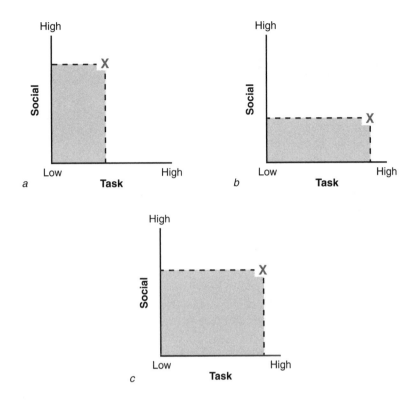

FIGURE 10.3   The team dynamics of cohesion.
Adapted, by permission, from B. Beswick, 2010, *Focused for soccer,* 2nd ed. (Champaign, IL: Human Kinetics), 177.

Task cohesion, guiding a team to play in a certain way, requires a skilled coach who has the following:

- Clear understanding of how she or he wants the game to be played
- Ability to inspire players to play that way
- Skills to define individual player job descriptions
- Tools to measure actual against expected performance
- Ability to give honest, clear feedback

Table 10.4 helps coaches assess their team's level of task cohesion. A large number of 'full understanding' answers indicates that the team's task cohesion is likely to be high in game situations. A large number of 'no understanding' answers gives the coach a wakeup call to take remedial action.

6. Social Cohesion

Building a team in harmony with their members' needs and feelings—with good social cohesion—is worthwhile because tasks have to be executed by people who have individual personalities, needs and wants.

TABLE 10.4   Assessing Your Team's Level of Task Cohesion

Coaching staff assesses how well the team understand how to deal with these game situations.

Game situation	Full understanding	Some or little understanding	No understanding
Each player knows his or her individual job			
Each player understands the job of his or her unit(e.g., back four, midfield, and so on)			
Each player knows the team game plan			
Each player is prepared at			
• Our kickoffs			
• Their kickoffs			
• Our goal kicks			
• Their goal kicks			
• Our corners			
• Their corners			
• Our free kicks			
• Their free kicks			
• Our throw-ins			
• Their throw-ins			
Each player understands how to play after we score			
Each player understands how to play after they score			
Each player knows his or her job when we are chasing the game			
Each player knows his or her job when we are defending a lead			
Each player understands how to play when we or they are down to 10 players			
Each player knows how to play when on a yellow card			

Adapted, by permission, from B. Beswick, 2010, *Focused for soccer*, 2nd ed. (Champaign, IL: Human Kinetics), 174.

Players have to be managed sensitively. Players today will not focus on performance if they believe that their feelings are not being taken care of. They require a resonant practice and playing environment that reflects and reinforces their feelings and an empathetic, positive and supportive coach. The creation of an effective team with good social cohesion is the responsibility of the coach and the other significant adults around the team. Table 10.5 offers coaches an exercise to check the level of social cohesion in their team.

To help develop greater social cohesion, coaches must pay attention to

- building the stability of the club,
- designing a player-centred programme,
- recruiting like-minded players,
- creating a caring environment,
- choosing socially adept staff,
- ensuring cultural tolerance,
- encouraging healthy relationships,
- developing player leadership and
- stimulating positive peer-group pressure.

Dealing With Nonselection

A critical moment that affects team cohesion occurs when a player is not selected and feels unfairly treated. The player should certainly be concerned, but both the coach and the player have a role in managing this situation by sending appropriate messages.

Coach Messages to Player

I have selected the best team for today.

This is why you are not included.

This is what you must work on.

Be ready on the bench.

Player Messages to Coach

I am disappointed but . . .

I accept a team decision and . . .

I will work on my game and . . .

I will be ready to help the team from the bench.

TABLE 10.5 Assessing Your Team's Level of Social Cohesion

Assess, as a coaching staff, how well your team score on the following situations.

Situation	True	Some truth	False
Players enjoy playing for our team.			
Very few players willingly leave our team.			
We have a high level of communication.			
It's hard work but fun to be in our team.			
Our team are never bored.			
Players on our team grow as people.			
Ethnic and cultural differences are respected on our team.			
Players respect, appreciate and encourage each other.			
We have stars but no isolates.			
We have a good record of developing player leadership.			
Honesty and trust are key words for us.			
We deal quickly with players who disrupt team harmony.			
Setbacks and defeats do not undermine morale.			
We surround our players with good, positive adults.			
Parents are part of the solution, not the problem.			
Togetherness is a key theme in our meetings.			
Relationships between coaches are positive and respectful.			

The higher the number of 'true' scores is, the more the team can be considered socially cohesive. A significant number of 'false' answers gives the coach a signal that action is needed.

Adapted, by permission, from B. Beswick, 2010, *Focused for soccer*, 2nd ed. (Champaign, IL: Human Kinetics), 176.

7. Psychological Stability

By setting standards for their team that are non-negotiable, coaches establish the rules of entry into their playing squad and subsequent membership. This approach reinforces team culture ('the way we do things round here') and contributes significantly to team cohesion.

Maintaining team cohesion through the ups and down of a season requires constant application. Coaches have to create a sense of psychological safety where setbacks cannot significantly damage cohesion. What players need is the knowledge that they can face the challenge of soccer with the coach's confidence and support at all times. Team cohesion is gained through trial and error, so players must be comfortable that they have the freedom to make mistakes and be corrected, though not humiliated, by the coach's response.

The creation of a psychological safety zone around the team allows the coach more time, energy and focus to deal with the external competitive challenges. Only when players (especially female players) feel safe will they pull together and flourish.

WINNING BY PUTTING THE TEAM FIRST

Coach Jason had been a successful professional player and understood very well the power of team cohesion. He had played for teams destroyed by selfishness and instability and had also played on teams who were united in their effort and achieved success.

So when he became director of coaching at a large youth soccer club, he made team cohesion a priority. Jason consulted me, and we developed a programme based on changing the mindset toward winning by building team cohesion throughout the club. Everyone would be involved and expected to reflect this new emphasis. The programme of change was built upon the following steps.

1. Put the team first.
In all relevant discussions and actions, the club would put the team's interests and needs first. Personal issues would be dealt with sensitively, but not at the expense of the team. Talented but selfish players (and parents) were confronted with a choice—change or go.

2. Highlight team effectiveness.
Instead of simply measuring and highlighting individual performance, the emphasis switched to team performance. Of course, goals would be celebrated, but so would assists, interceptions, saves made and so on. Effort would be rewarded as equally as talent.

3. Allow everybody to contribute.
Jason insisted on a policy of inclusion and encouraged coaches not only to give players responsibilities but also to find time for them to demonstrate their worth on the field. Development and results would have to happen in partnership.

4. Build respect.
Effective teamwork is based on respect and trust. The importance of a sound value system and respectful interpersonal relationships was stressed constantly. This went beyond understanding each other's roles and responsibilities to understanding each other's background and culture.

5. Coach leadership.
Trust within a team, like distrust, is a direct reflection of a team leader. Jason asked all coaches in the club to look in the mirror and ask themselves whether they modelled trust and integrity. Those coaches who did not put their team before their ego soon left.

6. Commit to excellence.

Being part of a team means accepting commitment, taking responsibility and being accountable. Coaches were required to teach these three foundations of character development alongside their work of developing talent. Jason instigated a visiting speakers programme that repeatedly emphasised the importance of character to personal and team success.

7. Pull the 'weeds'.

A 'weed' refuses to accept team guidelines and cannot move from a 'me' attitude. In the end weeds cannot be trusted and will damage the team, so coaches were asked to consider whether pulling the weeds out would give everyone else on the team a chance to grow. This part of the programme proved to be tough but necessary.

Naturally, Jason met some resistance, but many others shared his views. With Jason's determination the programme created a team-orientated and cohesive style of winning soccer throughout the club.

Chapter 11

SUMMONING MOMENTUM

When Manchester United played Swansea City at home in the FA Cup, the score was 1-1 with 10 minutes left. United were building momentum, and the crowd expected a winning goal. Whilst United focused on winning, Swansea focused on not losing. But then suddenly Fabio, the United fullback, was sent off for a dangerous tackle.

Both teams immediately changed their mindset—United to defend with 10 men, Swansea to seize the opportunity. As mindsets changed, the pattern of play altered. Swansea were now playing with their foot on the gas and United with their foot on the brake. Inevitably, with such a complete swing in momentum, possession and territory, Swansea scored the winner with two minutes left.

The *Oxford Dictionary of Sports Science and Medicine* (3rd ed., 2006) defines psychological momentum as

> The positive or negative change in cognition, affect, physiology and behaviour caused by an event, or series of events, that affects either the perceptions of the competitors or, perhaps, the quality of performance and the outcome of the competition. Positive momentum is associated with periods of competition, such as a winning streak, in which everything seems to go right for the competitor. In contrast, negative momentum is associated with periods, such as a losing streak, when everything seems to go wrong.

Playing soccer is a state of mind underpinned by physical power, technical skills and tactical intelligence. This state of mind is fluid, dynamic and open to both positive and negative influences. At any given point in the season or in a specific game, a team may be

- gaining momentum—'on a roll', 'on a streak';
- in full momentum—'riding the wave,' 'in the zone';
- losing momentum—'stemming the tide', 'out of sync' or
- regaining momentum—'kick starting', 'finding a rhythm'.

For coaches watching their team from the sideline, team momentum can be assessed by the answers to these questions.

- Are we playing with physical commitment?
- Do we have high tempo and energy?
- Are we dominating possession?
- Are we winning tackles, interceptions, headers?
- Is the game being mostly played in the opponent's half?
- Are we getting crosses into their penalty box?
- Have we had scoring opportunities?
- Are we ahead in the game?

For the coach who has positive answers to these questions, the likelihood is victory—if they can maintain the momentum. If the coach cannot answer positively, her or his major concern is changing the team's momentum from negative back into positive.

Teams are never stationary or fixed; they are always moving, however slowly, in a positive or negative direction. Momentum is gained and lost in bursts, pushing forward at one time and falling back at others. The team on top is the one able to summon and sustain periods of positive momentum, especially in the final phase of the game, and deal quickly with those periods when momentum falls back. Momentum, whether positive or negative, can be compared to a rolling snowball that begins small but, if unchecked, becomes large and forceful and capable of rolling over things in its way.

Coaches must recognise momentum as integral to their team's progress and become attuned to how their actions can create and sustain (or undermine) team momentum.

Building Background Momentum

Successful soccer clubs begin the process of building positive momentum long before the team take to the field at game time. They realise that if a positive culture of excellence is created and nurtured throughout the club, coaches and players have a much sounder foundation upon which to grow game momentum.

I contributed to the preparation of the Middlesbrough FC team who won the Carling Football League Cup. The game was won by the positive mindset and momentum that the team started the game with, scoring two goals in the first seven minutes.

Key background influences that we got right included the following:

- Preparation—avoiding overcoaching and overtraining
- Organisation—minimising distractions

- Selection—choosing a perfect blend and balance
- Game-day structure—being relaxed but positive
- Pregame meeting—playing an inspirational film clip
- Locker-room management—being upbeat and confident

Team psychological momentum, positive or negative, begins well before game time. Figure 11.1 shows the variety of elements within a soccer club that together shape a positive, enabling environment that allows players to feel confident to go out and play. This enabling context is based on doing things right—planning, organising practice, game preparation and so on—thus providing the momentum so that everyone believes that this club is going forward and is a good place to be.

The start of any Premier League soccer season in England is full of examples of momentum killers—a planned preseason tour that benefits the club commercially but doesn't allow players time to recover, individual players holding out for transfer requests and teams suddenly having to absorb three or four new players.

The tennis player Andre Agassi (2009) emphasised the power of momentum:

> Our best intensions are often thwarted by external forces—forces that we ourselves set in motion long ago. Decisions, especially bad ones, create their own kind of momentum, and the momentum can be a bitch to stop, as every athlete knows. Even when we vow to change, even when we sorrow and atone for our mistakes, the momentum of our past keeps carrying us down the wrong road. Momentum rules the world.

FIGURE 11.1 The foundations of team momentum.

The more the club, the players and the team commit positive actions in pursuit of a common aim, the more a buildup of belief will occur that all things are possible as positive momentum takes things forward.

Linking Mindset and Momentum

Mindset and momentum and are clearly linked; they feed each other. How a team think is how they play, and how they play shapes how they think. If a team are confident and assertive, they will be likely to build positive momentum—winning their challenges, controlling possession, playing in their opponent's half, creating more goal chances and so on. These results of being in positive momentum provide the evidence that strengthens confidence and gives the belief that they have the edge on their opponents and can win the game.

For the team in negative momentum, the evidence is that they are losing the contest, and, unless checked, this trend will quickly drain confidence and belief.

Similarly, the connection between momentum and energy is a vital component of soccer. The team winning the momentum battle will feel energetic and proactive and will play on the front foot. The team dealing with negative momentum can easily lose energy, become reactive and play on the back foot.

Of course, the better the game is and the more evenly matched the teams are, the more the momentum will shift from one team to the other. The great teams can exert positive momentum more frequently than the opposition can. The ability to do this is often a result of the relationship between the tactics and game plan set by the coach and the resultant mindset of the team. FC Barcelona are an example of the strength of this connection. Gerard Piqué, their outstanding centre-back, was inspired by the tactics laid down by former coach Pep Guardiola, as he described their style of play:

> A hounding, swarming eagerness to regain possession was one of the keys with Guardiola. We can take the ball from the other teams in two to five seconds. Maybe we try to score, then lose the ball—but we have it back in five seconds, and have a chance to score again. So finally the opponent was in a situation where he was defending all the time. And for us, maybe for our style of play we didn't need to defend a lot because in five seconds we can take the ball back. (Howard 2014, p S13)

The chain of events that direct momentum can occur as the following sequence:

- An event, positive or negative, occurs.
- The team change the way they think and feel.
- This leads to a change of behaviour.
- This leads to a change in performance.
- Momentum shifts from one team to another.
- The outcome of the game may change.

Sport psychologist Patrick Cohn (2008) illustrates a team change of mindset and momentum after they score a goal and then try to hold the lead:

> You stop playing the game you played to be in that position. And the moment you switch to trying not to screw up, you go from a very offensive mindset to a very defensive mindset. If you're focusing too much on the outcome, it's difficult to play freely. And now they're worried more about the consequences and what's going to happen than what they need to do right now.

As explained previously, momentum is created by a chain of events triggered by a significant occurrence. This can be positive or negative, either before or during the game. Coaching a game is about setting in motion events that trigger positive momentum (a decisive change of tactics or a key substitution, for example) and recognising and reacting to the negative triggers that can cause the team to decline into a downward spiral (see table 11.1).

A negative spiral often develops because of an initial mistake, which can be a powerful trigger. This first mistake sets in motion a thinking

TABLE 11.1 Triggers That Stimulate Mindset and Momentum

Positive momentum	Negative momentum
Scoring a goal	Conceding a goal
Feeling confident	Perceived lack of ability
Positive attitude	Opponents' reputation
Negative body language of opponents	Playing opponents of higher ability
Opponents' mistakes	Nerves and anxiety
Encouragement by teammates, captain, crowd, coach	Negative criticism
Team cohesion	Bad luck, mistakes, fatigue
Referee calls going your way	Referee decisions against you
Changing tactics substitutions	Complacency
Halftime used well	Halftime used badly

process and subsequent behaviours that are transformed step by step into negative momentum:

- Analysis—'Why did that happen?'
- Overthinking—'How do I make up for that?'
- Loss of focus—distracted from actual play
- Trying harder—loss of emotional control
- Making more mistakes—escalation
- Playing outside the game plan—desperation

When a team go into a negative spiral, they tend to lose focus, rush and make mistakes. One of the most common errors in soccer is to make one mistake, lose emotional control and concentration and then immediately make another mistake. Coaches must urge their players not to follow one mistake with a second and always seek to create a positive action after a negative. To prevent a negative spiral from developing, teams need to change an initial negative response to thinking, acting and behaving in a more assertive, positive manner. A simple strategy for calming the mind, refocusing on quality and rebuilding positive momentum is simply to ask the team to keep the ball for six passes before seeking to attack. This tactic slows down the game, calms the team, frustrates the opposition and can reverse the momentum of the game. Overcoming negative momentum thus builds resilience—the ability to bounce back from such incidents in the future.

Table 11.2 identifies the signs of a team mindset in a positive spiral, becoming increasingly optimistic and assertive, or a negative spiral, becoming pessimistic and fragile.

TABLE 11.2 **Signs of Positive and Negative Spirals**

Positive spiral	Negative spiral
Anticipating success	Anticipating failure
Sense of control	Feeling of threat
Increased confidence	Loss of confidence
High energy	Reduced energy
Feelings of invincibility	Feelings of helplessness
Optimism, thinking ahead	Distraction and loss of focus
Unafraid of risk	Avoiding responsibility
Team feeling like winners	Negative body language
Relationships improving	Excuses and blaming

Mistakes always happen, so coaches need strategies for dealing with them. Coaches have to determine their response to negative mistakes, such as errors made through loss of focus or poor decision making, and positive mistakes. Positive mistakes are usually signs of a team's intent to play. An attack-minded, front-foot strategy will create mistakes, but any negative effect is diluted by the surge of confidence that the team feel from their attacking mindset. The team forced to defend feel threatened, change the way they think and therefore feel and may start to make unforced errors. Coaches have to embrace positive mistakes as part of their teaching philosophy, ensuring as far as possible that they don't damage overall team momentum.

Managing and Monitoring Game Momentum

Most successful coaches and leaders on the field are able to reorganise and deal quickly with in-game momentum shifts. Critical situations include scoring or conceding a goal, a change of tactics, a change of personnel, injuries, bad refereeing calls and the perception that the opposing team are weakening.

Momentum changes occur in most games for any number of reasons. By recognising when they tend to occur and what causes them, coaches can begin to develop an effective coping strategy (see table 11.3). When I was advising the University of South Carolina women's team, we played a game of what-if in practice. I called out a game momentum change, and they called back a positive response. In the game that evening the team conceded a goal in the 10th minute. After a few seconds the players heard a shout from a smart member of the team, 'No problem, 80 minutes still to play!' In a calm manner the team regained momentum and won the game!

Several factors can contribute to a successful coping strategy:

- Senior player leadership taking decisions on the field
- Dealing with the shift rationally and not reacting emotionally
- Staying in the present, taking no time for guilt or anxiety
- Changing a negative into a positive, quickly finding a way back
- Continuing to do the simple but important things
- Keeping composed and staying strong in the game

There are however, three important phases of the game where the coach can seek to exert maximum influence on team momentum.

1. Starting Well

When a team run on the field they have collectively established a mind-set that will influence momentum early in the game. The evidence on which this mindset is based will be factors such as the last result, the week's preparation, the team selection, the return from injury of a star player and so on.

TABLE 11.3 Controlling Momentum

This three-stage exercise teaches teams how to understand momentum and how to change it in their favour.

1. IN CONTROL: THE TEAM WATCH A SIX-MINUTE FILM CLIP IN WHICH THEY ARE CLEARLY IN CONTROL OF THE GAME.	
Questions	**Likely responses**
• What is happening when you are in control? • What does it look like, feel like, sound like? • How are the crowd—(if at home?) • or • How are the crowd – (if away from home?)	Good shape, all players doing their jobs Urgency in play, playing on the front foot Lots of communication Possession kept for good periods Discipline in defence Confidence and adventure in attack Away crowd quiet
2. OUT OF CONTROL: THE TEAM WATCH A SIX-MINUTE FILM CLIP IN WHICH THEY ARE CLEARLY OUT OF CONTROL OF THE GAME.	
Questions	**Likely responses**
• What has changed? • Why has it changed? • What does it look like, feel like, sound like now? • How are the crowd— (if at home?) • or • How are the crowd – (if away from home?)	Loss of shape and discipline Loss of focus Mistakes—ball given away easily Loss of emotional control and panic Hiding and avoiding responsibility Less communication and leadership Crowd on our back
3. REGAINING CONTROL: BRAINSTORM WITH THE TEAM.	
Questions	**Likely responses**
• What do you need to do? • Individually? • Collectively? • As captain, seniors, leaders?	Settling down, being calm and patient Positive attitudes, taking responsibility Positive communication—talking up! All players focusing on doing their jobs well Keeping team shape in defence and attack Prioritising possession (six passes) Everybody wanting the ball Playing in their half to give them problems Staying disciplined—not giving momentum back Keeping it simple

Many coaches understand the importance of this early mindset on momentum and practise a start-of-game phase. For example, many teams away from home elect (if possible) to kick off, kick long to the corner and then squeeze up to ensure that the early play is in the opponent's half. The more confident teams simply keep the ball and demonstrate to the opposition their confidence in possession.

Few teams at higher levels dominate from the start, and momentum is often shared during the first half (refer to figure 11.2). During this time the coach should be reflective rather than proactive. Unless intervention is absolutely necessary, the coach should be preparing for the vital opportunity to intervene at halftime with the aim of either maintaining or regaining positive momentum.

2. Halftime

Of particular importance to the coach is halftime—a challenge to both the coach who is leading and the coach who is losing. A winning momentum is often lost at halftime by poor coaching, especially when the coach is more anxious than the team, and manages to replace the team's confidence with anxiety. Equally, the team going into halftime with negative momentum can seize the impetus if the coach intervenes in an insightful way by dispelling anxiety with an optimistic and confident approach to the second half of the game.

Losing 2-0 at halftime, one particular coach was about to explode with his team. Then the usually quiet statistician remarked that four times already that season the team had come back from two goals down at halftime to get a result. The coach walked into the locker-room with a changed mindset, reminded the team of their four previous recoveries and challenged them to make it five. Team mindset went from negative to positive, from pessimistic to optimistic, and game momentum completely reversed as they started playing with confidence and aggression, eventually winning 3-2.

A common and helpful coaching tactic is to challenge the team to win the second half, thus helping to build a mindset of resilience and mental toughness.

The halftime period provides the most significant opportunity the soccer coach gets to change momentum. Using the evidence of the first half, the coach can make three key decisions to influence mindset and momentum:

1. Change personnel—will a new player or players influence the game?

2. Change tactics—will a shape adjustment create better defence or offense?

3. Change attitude—can we rebuild optimism and belief, and therefore renew energy?

In a famous European Cup Final the Liverpool manager Rafael Benitez, losing 0-3 to Milan at halftime, changed personnel, tactics and attitude. The momentum of the game swung immediately in Liverpool's favour, and they went on to win and become European Champions.

In an infamous Premier League game, former Hull FC manager Phil Brown used halftime to keep his losing team on the field and berate them in front of their fans. The plan backfired on the manager. The team felt humiliated, lost momentum and lost the game. The manager lost his job!

3. Final Stages of the Game

Gerard Houllier, a member of FIFA's Technical Group at the 2014 World Cup in Brazil, gave a clear indication of the importance of gaining momentum at the end of the game:

> The tempo, the pace of the World Cup has never been faster. The level and intensity of the drama has never been so high. Five of the round of 16 games were not decided in normal time, a record (the first time since 1938).

> Nearly a quarter of the goals have been scored in the final 15 minutes. Subs play an important part: 29 goals have been scored by subs, a record. You normally have 10 per cent of goals scored by subs. (Winter, 2014 p S10)

So the most decisive phase in a game is often the final stages. At this point, any momentum shift from positive to negative should provoke a reaction from the coach. The coach wants to alert the team to the danger and get them back into the positive as soon as possible. Several strategies can be effective:

- Becoming visible and demonstrative
- Urging the team on vocally
- Signalling a tactical change
- Creating a break in the game (occasionally outside the rules and spirit of the game)
- Sending the substitutes to warm up (a subtle message to the team playing)
- Making an important substitution.

Mapping Game Momentum

Mapping game momentum is a technique that coaches are increasingly using to understand the swings of the game and the effects that these momentum changes can have on team mindset and performance. With a greater understanding and awareness of how and why momentum alters at critical points in the game, the coach can make crucial interventions that can help the team.

In the game represented by the momentum map (or graph) shown in figure 11.2, the following events occurred:

- Red team had positive momentum for the first 30 minutes but could not score.
- Momentum switched suddenly after 30 minutes. Blue team dominated the rest of the half and scored two goals. (This change of momentum was caused by a tactical change by Blue team coach.)
- Halftime was important for both coaches:
  - Blue team wanted to maintain the positive momentum established.
  - Red team needed to find a way to regain momentum and come back from 0-2.
- In the second half Blue team started well, but the changes made at halftime by Red team coach (personnel and tactical) gradually change momentum.
- Red team scored two goals to tie the game but made the mistake of relaxing after the equalising goal and allowing Blue team to regain momentum for the final phase of game during extra time.

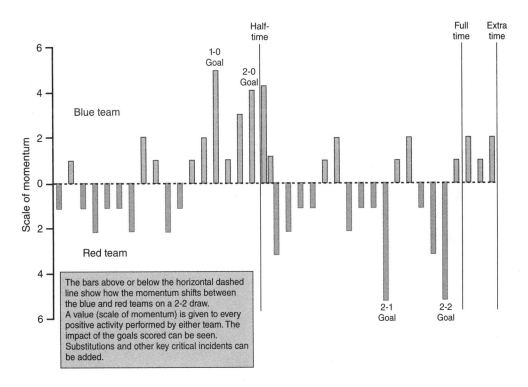

FIGURE 11.2 An example of mapping game momentum.

HOW THE COACH DEVELOPED A
COPING STRATEGY TO SHAPE TEAM MOMENTUM

Michael, a boys U14 coach, was concerned about the fragile nature of his team. Instead of dealing with the highs and lows of the game, the team seemed to give up positive momentum too easily and then struggle to regain it. Michael described to me a team who

- started nervously and showed opponents too much respect,
- were more concerned with the outcome than the process,
- saw every decision against them as a sign they would lose,
- after conceding a goal, might concede again and
- after scoring, would defend rather than quickly go for a second goal.

This team had a weak collective mindset and a lack of game management coping strategies. The coach and I agreed the following programme:

- Create and rehearse game scenarios in practice—if this happens, then we will . . .
- Establish a pregame routine that ignores opponents and boosts team self-image.
- Develop leaders within the team who will take charge in critical moments.
- Regularly practise and emphasise the importance of positive self-talk using game situations.
- Set up practice games in which the coach could call time-outs if he saw negative momentum setting in.
- Highlight and illustrate positive momentum shifts—a good tackle, save, interception, pass or shot on goal.
- Focus entirely on the process and reduce anxiety, on and off the field, about the results.
- Accept refereeing decisions and get on with the game.
- Stress that the team never rest on 1-0 and always go for the second goal.

These measures, supported by some useful analysis of game films, built a coping strategy in the team. This process created a more positive game mentality, produced longer periods of positive momentum and allowed their talent to shine.

Chapter 12

HANDLING PRESSURE

Working with teams from grassroots to international level has shown me that a winning team need to have both high levels of talent and great mental strength. I have also learned that at elite level, differences in talent between teams become less significant and winning the big games becomes a test of a team's mental strength to handle the pressure involved.

When Steve Round left Everton to join Manchester United as assistant manager, he shared with me the increased pressure he immediately felt:

> The most noticeable difference between Everton and United was the level of pressure. What I realised instantly was how big a club it was and how it took a special kind of coach and player to cope with the added pressure.
>
> It began with the sideshow, the commercial, media and PR responsibilities that always threatened to get in the way of playing the game. Then there was dealing with the expectations of a 75,000 crowd and global following. Defeat seemed like a disaster and of course every team in the league wants the scalp of Man U. No game was ever easy and at times it seemed like pressure, pressure, pressure. But then that's what the job is— handling pressure.

A pressure situation in soccer can generally be characterised as a time of great uncertainty, when the game can go either way, and a time of importance, when the stakes are high.

Recognising Pressure

Players recognise the effect of pressure by their physiological responses— rapid breathing, sweaty palms, butterflies and so on. Table 12.1 shows how the pressure of game importance and uncertainty increases as a player moves through levels of competition.

TABLE 12.1 Ten Stages of Soccer Pressure

Steps	Importance	Uncertainty
1. Playing alone 2. Playing with friends 3. Playing for a team 4. Playing regionally 5. Playing nationally 6. Playing professionally 7. Becoming a star 8. Playing in big games 9. Playing in the World Cup 10. Playing in the World Cup Final	Low High	Low High

Teams with a strong, competitive mindset are high on passion, the everyday motivation to learn and prepare to be winners, and high on toughness, the ability to endure pressure, stay in the game and persist until the final whistle.

The winning combination that achieves most consistently is sufficient talent driven by a passionate and tough mindset. Teams with talent but a weak mindset will always threaten to win but mostly succumb to the pressure and lose. Teams with less talent but a powerful mindset will refuse to be victims and often drive themselves into winning situations. The ability to handle pressure confers a key competitive advantage to a team.

Winning teams defeat performance anxiety with a tough individual and collective mindset that refuses to slide from positive confidence into negative anxiety. Toughness is not a question of size or strength but an attitude, a determined and focused state of mind that can be developed. Top teams have mental and emotional skills that allow disciplined thinking and action under pressure and fatigue. Mental strength is the final gateway to top performance.

Teams competing at the elite level, such as in the English Premier League, have to deal with a variety of pressure scenarios—leading the league, fighting a slump, losing a key player, changing the coach and so on. Arsene Wenger, the manager of Arsenal FC, recognised this: 'The only thing we have learned from these first six months is that the team who has the greatest emotional stamina and resolve will win. It could be a league of the mentally strong' (Wilson 2011b, p 56).

Arsene understands that champions need to maintain an optimum mindset throughout the rollercoaster of a season. When physical, technical and tactical skills are matched, then the team who are mentally stronger will usually prevail. Pressure is inevitable, so the defining characteristic of teams who win regularly is their ability to thrive in pressure-packed situations where everything is on the line.

> Pressure is nothing more than the shadow of a great opportunity.

Perceiving Pressure

The demands of soccer exert five key pressures that can affect the mind-set of teams.

1. **Performance pressure**—the expectations of others and the consequences of defeat leading to anxiety and fear.

2. **Competition pressure**—making decisions and executing skills when challenged and under fatigue leading to confusion, lack of confidence and errors.

3. **Time pressure**—the need to respond quickly throughout the game and at the end of game when the clock is ticking down leading to anxiety and frustration.

4. **Distraction pressure**—the crowd, the noise and incidents on the field distracting attention and leading to a loss of focus.

5. **Emotional pressure**—refereeing decisions, mistakes and frustration with teammates leading to anger and loss of composure.

The mindset of a team can be strengthened or weakened by how they assess the challenges awaiting them. This definition of the situation shapes and drives subsequent performance.

> When everything comes together for highly successful teams they know they are going to win before they step out into the field. This knowing is the most powerful state of mind for any team.
>
> Bill Walsh (2009)

Four-time Olympic Gold Medal winner Michael Johnson is widely regarded as one of the most successful athletes of all time. He acknowledges that his psychological approach to competition was crucial to his sustained success on the track. Meticulous planning and preparation complemented by intense focus allowed him to perform consistently even when under extreme pressure. Johnson's approach was to train his mind to be disciplined and so deal with the intense pressure of competition. His definition of pressure removed any negative connotations in his mind.

All performance starts in the mind before a game as teams and players seek answers to these questions:

- What exactly is the challenge we face today?
- What do we know of our opponents?
- What is our record against them?
- How strong is our team?
- Are we well prepared?
- Who will lead us into battle?

Moment of Truth

The moment of truth for any player or team is when they cross the white line into a major competitive arena. It is at this moment when they feel the full pressure of the occasion. Here are some observations of the thinking that underpins the way that pressure affects performers and is then dealt with.

The pressure of performing live—the time is now!

A moment of no return—we cannot defer any longer.

A feeling of being alone to fight a personal battle.

The internal dialogue sways between confidence and anxiety.

Rapid heartbeat, muscular tension, sweaty palms, nausea.

The world awaits a response—fighter or victim?

Hard-earned experience is drawn upon:

- A lifetime of self-doubt
- Years of struggle
- Years of conquering fears every day
- Years of overcoming failure
- The discipline of repetition and habits

Emotional courage is summoned:

- Thinking, 'I can'
- Feeling, 'I will'
- Release of positive energy

The first step is crucial—years of training crystallised into a single moment:

- First touch
- First header
- First tackle
- Habits take over—preparation is everything.
- The crowd respond.
- The player responds—'I did it'. What better feeling?
- The experience is banked for next time.

- Do I feel confident?
- Do I want to do this?
- What are the risks?
- What are the expectations of others?
- What are the consequences of failure?

The answers to these questions define the situation as perceived by the players, thus also defining their level of confidence and subsequent game behaviour. A positive definition of the situation is a frame of reference that can carry teams through difficult games because they think and behave like fighters, not victims. The task of coaches, supported by sport psychologists, is to help each player win the internal dialogue and overcome the weaker self.

Young players, especially girls, hold five common though irrational perceptions:

1. My self-worth is on the line in this game.
2. I must perform to please others.
3. I must be perfect.
4. The world must always be fair.
5. I must always hate my opponent.

When Gary Kirsten coached the Indian cricket team to World Cup victory in India, the team had a major external pressure, the expectations of one billion people! Gary eased the pressure on the team by changing the picture and having them visualise one billion friends walking hand in hand with them to victory! The key to handling pressure is seeing challenge as a chance to shine, not a reason to fail.

The process by which a team agree a collective mindset towards a game begins when each player assesses her or his ability to meet the challenge. All players can then be influenced by the actions and words of senior team leaders, the coach's positive definition of the situation and any additional motivational techniques, such as a film or visiting speaker. From this process a collective response to the challenge emerges.

A winning mindset handles pressure by ensuring that positive values, attitudes and emotions bring behaviour that helps to conquer anxiety and fear. Coaches and sport psychologists need to teach players to define the competitive situation positively through using the skills of positive mental self-regulation, becoming comfortable with being intense but not tense.

> Man is not worried by real problems so much as by his imagined anxieties about real problems.
>
> Epictetus
> Greek philosopher

Managing Performance Upwards Through Comfort Zones

Performance anxiety—wanting to do well though fearing failure, wanting to please while being unsure and so on—often forces teams who cannot handle pressure into a comfort zone. A team in this situation will exhibit a lower level of performance in which anxiety is reduced to neutral and the perceived sense of risk is small. The comfort zone adopted reflects the collective mindset of the team. A team who participate in soccer at a recreational level (see figure 12.1, comfort zone level 1) will stay there unless a coach persuades them of the need to be more competitive. They need to work harder to achieve this, to break through a degree of discomfort up to the next level. The process then has to be repeated as the team assimilate the pressure and are able to move on.

Three stages are important:

Comfort zone, level 1—avoid pressure, unwilling to commit to discomfort, love excuses, seek low risk, exert low effort, avoid responsibility, give up easily

Comfort zone, level 3 (challenge zone)—beginning to handle pressure, willing to commit to discomfort, cope with higher risk, make great effort and take responsibility

Comfort zone, level 5 (warrior zone)—thrive on pressure, need to commit, accept discomfort, don't see risk, demand high effort, seek feedback and take total responsibility

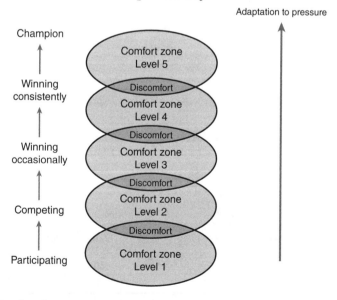

FIGURE 12.1   Comfort zones.

Top teams always face new and fast-moving competitive challenges, so they never relax into a comfort level. They win, set more challenging goals, suffer the discomfort of striving to achieve them and then repeat the process, driving on through the interim periods of discomfort and anxiety and never settling to stay in a comfort zone. Such responses separate teams with fighter mentality from those with victim mentality.

Removing Fear to Dispel Pressure

Pressure only exists when anxiety overwhelms confidence and becomes fear in a player's mind. Not allowing this to happen is a great mental attribute seen in successful players, teams and coaches.

Pete Carroll, the head coach of the NFL Super Bowl 48 Champions, the Seattle Seahawks, acknowledged the influence of fear in his coaching philosophy:

> In my time as a coach I've learned that possibly the greatest detractor from high performance is fear. Fear you are not prepared, fear you are in over your head, fear that you are not worthy, and ultimately fear of failure. If you can eliminate that fear—not through arrogance or just wishing difficulties away but through hard work and preparation—you will put yourself in an incredibly powerful position to take on the challenges you face.

> Ideally we want to create an atmosphere or a culture where our players can perform in the absence of fear. Achieving this means finding ways to prove to players that they can rely on themselves and their teammates to perform at the highest level in the face of any challenge—even losing. (Carroll 2010, p 177–8)

Carroll recognised that losing often stems from fear and that fear, left unchecked, can result in a losing streak. When fear and losing go hand in hand,

- communication decreases,
- criticism and blame increase,
- respect decreases,
- isolation increases,
- focus turns inward,
- rifts widen and inequities grow,

- initiative decreases,
- aspirations diminish and
- negativity spreads.

Teams and coaches must learn to distinguish between 'good fear' and 'bad fear'. Good fear means acknowledging that things could go wrong but knowing that you have done the detailed, hard work of thorough preparation and given yourself the best chance possible. Bad fear means expecting things to go wrong, forgetting learning, avoiding responsibility, seeking excuses and looking for a way out.

Properly harnessing good fear allows a team to reach an optimum performance zone, confident in their belief they can win but with sufficient controlled anxiety to know that they must give their best effort.

Coaches at all levels need to understand the causes of fear in their teams and then find strategies to remove them. In my experience five key strategies can lower anxiety.

1. **The coach models optimism and at all times looks, behaves and communicates in a positive manner**. The image and actions of the coach tells the players how they should be feeling. They will be pessimistic and negative if the coach is locked in a state of fear or is ego dependent on a win. Young coaches reach an essential development threshold when they become bigger than any one result and thus are never frightened of a defeat.

2. **Coaches must imbue their team with belief, not fear**. If a team become threatened with the consequences should they not perform well, they often self-destruct when the game is on the line. The consequences of failure become an overwhelming distraction under pressure. Teams are more likely to rise to a belief-filled challenge set by a coach than respond with any positivity to the anxiety-inducing threats of a coach desperate to win. Jürgen Klinsmann, head coach of the USA Men's National Soccer Team, demonstrated a lack of fear as a player and as a coach:

> I think expectations and the word *pressure* is an excuse because if you learn how to do your job, it's no problem. It's actually a pleasure. If you ignore all the sideshow and just focus on your job, on your game, then you will have no problems with the fact there's pressures or high expectations. I think actually you enjoy it far more. And you need to enjoy your job. (*Sunday Times*, 2011, 11 September, Sport p 13)

3. **Coaches must fight negativity with positivity based on the absolute knowledge, transmitted to the team, that they have been fully prepared for each game**. Many top players have shared with me the connection between their confidence at game time and the thoroughness of their preparation. To be unprepared is to invite anxiety and then fear. Thus pressure is increasingly felt.

   Tim Grover, a strength and conditioning specialist, came to understand the relationship between the hard work of preparation and dispelling fear when he worked with top athletes:

   > That's the trademark of a dangerous competitor: He doesn't have to know what's coming because whatever you show him, he's ready. No fear of failure.

   > That's not about the myth of 'positive thinking'. It's about the hard work and preparation that goes into knowing everything there is to know, letting go of your fear and insecurities and trusting your ability to handle any situation. (Grover 2013, p 114)

4. **The coach must reduce individual player fear by insisting on team collective responsibility, that they win and lose together as a team**. This approach reduces blame, removes the burden from any individual player's shoulders, encourages shared ownership of results and aids future learning.

5. **To prevent fear from accumulating in the minds of players, a critical moment occurs in the locker-room after a defeat**. The team depend on the coach to tell them how to feel about the game and their performance. If the coach misjudges the game summary that she or he delivers to the team, fear can remain embedded and be carried forward into future performances. However if the coach is able to demonstrate emotionally stable body language and speech, a disappointed but calm demeanour, that positives as well as negatives were on display, hope for the future and a positive team message in conclusion, then fear is removed and the team can look forward to practice and the next game without any burden of accumulated anxiety.

   Top coaches do not fear losing or allow it to undermine the mindset of their team. Their personal strength allows them to remove the fear from their team and minimise a major source of pressure.

Coping With Pressure

Teams can't be expected to play well under pressure if they have not been prepared to handle game situations. It is not compulsory to feel pressure. Well-prepared teams can easily handle the pressure of the moment.

After winning the 2014-15 Premier League title, Chelsea's mid-field player, Cesc Fabregas said of his manager, Jose Mourinho:

> You need someone behind it all, which is the manager, who every single day makes you be at the top of your game. He just loves winning. I'm not just saying other managers I have played under don't, but he has some edge that goes above anyone else I have ever been with. The mentality shows every single training session and every single game. I now understand why he has won what he has won in his career.

(Hughes, M. 'Obsessive Desire to Win has Made Mourinho the Best, says Fabregas' in *The Times*, 2015, 5 May, Sport p 64).

Good coaches fully appreciate the direct link between proper preparation to a state of game readiness and the resultant quality of performance on game day. Seeing the link physically is easy, but if the coach demands game-day mental strength and disciplined thinking under pressure and fatigue, then this too must be rehearsed continuously in practice. Teams cannot practise without challenge or competition and then be expected to deal with such pressures on game day. Figure 12.2 shows how coaches can help players identify their own particular pressure points as part of the postgame performance feedback process. Using this exercise, coach and player can work together on improving the player's capacity to cope.

Make Pressure a Part of Practice

The practice-field environment is different from the game environment with its many unpredictable variables. The key to handling pressure in games is to replicate that pressure as nearly as possible in training. Coaches must integrate competitive and challenging situations within practice and simulate game scenarios. The more that practices resemble game day, including coping with unexpected situations, the better the team will cope with game pressure.

Practice must combine physical conditioning, skill acquisition by building a range of techniques and stress adaptation by increasing the demands on the player and team.

When done well, this approach increases player awareness of potential pressure situations and provides a range of tools to deal with them. Practice performed in this way limits likely game pressure by increasing awareness, reducing anxiety and increasing confidence.

Figure 12.2 Postgame Performance Feedback Sheet

Name:	
Date:	
Game:	
1. What, if anything, stressed you today?	
2. How did you experience any stress (thoughts, actions, physically)?	
3. How aroused were you (pregame, warm-up, game)?	
4. How did you manage any stress?	
5. How was your self-talk? Describe.	
6. What did you learn today?	
7. What mental training methods work for you?	
8. What did you enjoy today?	
9. How would you rate your performance (scale of 1–10 where 1 is terrible, 5 is OK, 10 is great)?	
10. How do you feel now (tired, OK, ready to go)?	

Note: Coaches or sport psychologists can modify this sheet to suit the age and performance level of their team. The exercise can be written or completed by short interviews.

Coaches can ensure that their teams practice under pressure by

- simulating a crowd effect by adding noise, distractions and so on,
- increasing the consequences of not performing well,
- favouring the opposition,
- reducing the time available and
- increasing complexity.

One coach I observed created a pressure scenario by combining a game with physical conditioning. The squad played a 12-minute game that included specific instructions for both teams (for example, 12 minutes left in the game and Red team leading 1-0, so Reds defend the lead and Blues try to equalise). The players then broke off for a 6-minute circuit-training session at the side of the field. After repeating this process three times, the coach evaluated their ability to handle pressure under fatigue.

Players with a warrior mentality welcome intensity in practice. They love practicing and seeing the improvement by pushing themselves as hard as possible. They also get annoyed when they think that they got nothing out of a poor practice session. This self-imposed pressure during the week is the perfect preparation for handling pressure on game day.

© skynesher/iStock.com

Physical training is a key element in adapting to the increasing demands of stress and coping with game pressure.

    Soccer is a game of 95 per cent preparation and 5 per cent performance. The whole of England remembers being one minute from failing to qualify for the 2002 World Cup. Then, in the deciding game against Greece in October 2001, well into stoppage time, David Beckham stepped up to take a free kick 25 yards from goal—last chance saloon! The pressure on David must have been enormous, but he could handle it because he was fully prepared. He always took a bag of balls out early before practice started, and he would have made at least 20 shots from that distance on many occasions—adding up to a memory of thousands of shots from that position. David felt confident because his body knew what to do. That confidence overcame the external pressure of the moment. David relaxed and scored a memorable goal.

    I came across an excellent description of this coping with pressure by Jeff Wilkins, an NFL kicker, in Selk (2009, p VII)

> The thing that all reporters get wrong when they ask me about 'pressure' after the game is that, in that one moment, there is no pressure. When I try to explain why, they can't fathom it, but I've been there a thousand times before. In every practice I see myself executing flawlessly, I know the feeling of being

calm and aggressive at the same time—where my mind has a pinpoint process on the one thing I need to do to be successful. In my mind I've practised that kick a thousand times.

The doubts everyone is curious about, wondering whether they creep into my mind, have no room in my head because I practise controlling my thoughts the same way I practise nailing down my technique. It all becomes routine, and mental toughness is what brings everything together.

Incorporating pressure in practice will both reveal and build each player's

- level of self-belief,
- strength of self-discipline,
- reliability of emotional control,
- intensity of competitive fire and
- ability to show leadership.

As the screw tightens, players either choke, cope or thrive (see table 12.2). Regular doses of intensity and stressful challenge in practice will see players at first learning to survive, then deal with and finally overcome pressure.

Bill Belichick, the coach of the New England Patriots, was recently rated NFL Coach of the Decade. Described in Lavin's book (2005), Belichick explained the team's success:

The biggest change came when we racked up the expectations and competitiveness of practice. Players had to pay attention and focus to survive and we saw both physical and mental development. Hard work is not a coaching strategy but a consequence of putting players in a practice environment that is competitive and performance focused every day.

TABLE 12.2   Coping and Fighter or Victim Mentality

Vulnerable	Coping	Thriving
Unsure that he or she can succeed	Confident in ability	Loves the challenge
Needs to win to avoid failure	Focuses only on performance	Unafraid, will take risks
Fears being judged	Doesn't see the crowd	Feeds off the crowd
Fears failing	Accepts possible failure	Sees opportunity to shine
Feels out of control	Stays in control	Loves being in control
Hides from pressure	Stays with the pressure	Commands the situation
Not sure he or she should be here	Accepts the situation	No other place to be
Victim ←		→ Fighter

Experience Counts

After not selecting David Beckham for the England National Team for a whole year, Coach Steve McClaren reintroduced David into the team. Steve's reasoning was that the team weren't handling the pressure of international football well and David's presence in the locker-room would calm them down. An experienced senior player with no fear of pressure can be a strong influence on a team.

Coaches should provide a series of competitive hurdles that players must pass through to toughen them up for first-team play. In this way players and teams

- learn to embrace pressure, not fear it,
- confront pressure rather than hide from it,
- build a range of coping responses,
- learn to think and act tough,
- maintain focus on the process, not the outcome,
- develop competitive toughness,
- set aspirational goals,
- understand that preparation equals confidence,
- learn not to get distracted and
- develop solid preperformance routines.

Make Perception of Pressure Positive

For female soccer players, the key stressors are poor performance and difficult relationships with coaches, teammates, parents and spectators. Because female players under pressure have a tendency to ruminate and beat themselves up, coaches need to be proactive in helping them change their perception of the situation from negative to positive.

Coaches must watch out for disengagement, venting, social isolation, aggression and so on. Several coping strategies can be effective:

- Team social support systems to share the pain
- Positive thinking and self-talk
- Working harder to overcome the stress
- Positive reappraisal and developing a new action plan
- Letting go and moving on.

Giacobbi et al. (2004) concluded their work on stress-coping strategies for female student athletes by stating,

Their coping strategies moved in three phases. Firstly they turned to family and teammates for emotional support and then they began to use more cognitive forms of coping which helped them to see stress as a challenge that offered potential benefits. Finally they developed a personal strategy that worked for them to deal with their stress.

The mental toughness to handle pressure is clearly a limiting factor in the development of players and teams. Such toughness can be developed if coaches regularly inject periods of intensity and stress at practice, allowing players to adapt to and deal with pressure-inducing situations. Only then can coaches expect disciplined thinking and action under pressure on game day.

Building a Fighter Mentality

Of all the teams I have worked with, Manchester United best demonstrated fighter mentality in 1999, a peak performance year. Dominated by two classic fighters, manager Sir Alex Ferguson and captain Roy Keane, the squad enjoyed being challenged and were willing to work hard every day to ensure that they achieved their need to win all the time. They saw pressure as a chance to shine, and they understood that the price to be paid was intense focus every day at practice. Nowhere else have I seen such a willingness by players to challenge each other when the play was poor. Roy Keane stood out as the kind of great player who made all the players round him better because of his demands for the team to meet consistent, high standards. Not even a surprise setback could turn this team into victims. They could be beaten, but they were never conquered.

A coaching environment designed to maximise a young player's ability to handle pressure has to incorporate a strong element of challenge. Coaches concerned with continuous development must provide toughness training to teach young players how to drive through comfort zones. Coaches should never accept a victim mentality in their players. Becoming successful can be uncomfortable at times, but toughness allows talent to flourish at the top levels.

Coaches can take 10 steps to build fighter mentality in their players.

1. Challenge players every day.
2. Set high expectations.
3. Make everything competitive.
4. Increase the complexity of drills.
5. Have players practise while they are fatigued.
6. Practise at game speed.

© Photoshot

Coaches help their players develop a fighter mentality, allowing them to face challenges head-on.

7. Do not accept excuses.
8. Demand discipline and execution.
9. Observe, evaluate and correct.
10. Make players accountable.

The limiting factor for most young players is not talent, but toughness. Coaching environments must incorporate mental toughness alongside physical, technical and tactical development. Such competitive toughness is defined by sport psychologist James Loehr (1994) as 'the ability to consistently perform toward the upper range of your talent and skill regardless of the competitive circumstances'.

Toughness is learned and built on these elements:

- A foundation of good fitness, diet and rest and recovery
- Technical mastery—technique equals freedom
- Emotional strength and control—tough thinking leads to tough actions

TABLE 12.3 Illustrative Trigger Card

A card designed by a player that describes her or his best 'performer self'. The player reads it before training and before matches to reduce anxiety and boost confidence.

I deserve to be on the field.
This is my day.
I am relaxed yet ready.
I know my job.
My first touch will be good.
This is my day.
I will seize the moment.
Mistakes will not deter me.
There is nowhere else I would rather be.
I will make this my day.
I will be the player who makes the difference.

- Creating a 'performer self'—changing personality from normal real self to a performer self, becoming a tough, competitive player on the field (see table 12.3)

Adopting a cognitive coping strategy of creating a performer self can be an especially important transition for women, because it allows them the psychological freedom to be more assertive and demanding on the field than they would feel comfortable with in their everyday life.

The personal trainer to many of America's top athletes, Tim Grover, is clear on the toughness needed to deal with pressure:

Pressure can bust pipes, but it can also make diamonds. If you take the negative view, it will crush you; now you're in an 'I can't do this' frame of mind. But the positive view is that pressure is a challenge that will define you; it gives you the opportunity to see how much you can take, how hard you can go. Stress keeps you sharp, it challenges you in ways you never imagined and forces you to solve issues and manage situations that send weaker people running for cover. You can't succeed without it. Your level of success is defined by how well you embrace it and manage it. (Grover 2013, p 102–103)

COACHING A YOUNG TEAM TO HANDLE PRESSURE

All teams face some pressure, but there is a step change at about 15 years of age when the game begins to be taken more seriously. So I was not surprised when Coach Dan sought my advice on his U16 boys team who were not handling pressure well. Suddenly, a team who had enjoyed playing soccer had gone from coping to victim mentality, showing a loss of enjoyment, an increase in anxiety, a decline in active engagement and an increase in making excuses and blaming.

Having identified the behavioural signs, I asked Dan to reflect on the causes. Where was the pressure coming from? He identified a change in external pressure on the boys; parents, teachers and friends were now making them aware that if they were successful at soccer, rewards could be coming in the form of scholarships or professional careers. We agreed that the outcome, standing out as a talented player and winning, had suddenly become more important than the process, enjoying the game alongside pursuing individual and team excellence.

Dan defined two key actions: (1) reinforce that playing well and winning were important and (2) teach the team to deal with the resultant pressure.

We agreed on the following steps:

- Get enjoyment back on the agenda—let pleasure defeat the pressure.
- Blend together enjoyment and working hard.
- Teach players to focus on controllables and not waste time or energy on uncontrollables.
- Emphasise the process, not the outcome, and let the wins come.
- Set performance goals, not outcome goals.
- Improve players' mistake management skills.
- Position parents at least three metres from the touchline during games.
- Interpret results in a positive way by crediting the effort, learning and progress even in a loss.
- Avoid getting too high after a win or too low after a defeat.

I also suggested that Dan find a way to let the parents share in his postgame analysis and therefore reduce parental pressure on the players. He came up with a clever solution, putting his game review comments into a short e-mail that he circulated soon after the game. Parents welcomed this summary, and it changed many negative perceptions to a more positive and less pressurised viewpoint. Interestingly, Dan believed that this exercise alone made him a more thoughtful and better coach.

All these initiatives combined to create a more positive mentality in and around the team, and the inevitable pressure was brought under control. Dan and his U16 team had a successful, and happy, season!

Chapter 13

OVERCOMING ADVERSITY

A key moment for a sport psychologist is being introduced to a team for the first time. I usually have a five-minute speech ready along these lines:

> Hi! It's a real pleasure for me to be asked to work with you. It's also an honour because I respect the people in this room. You do what I wasn't able to. You cross the white line every day and face the many, many challenges to being a top performer. You could be at home watching a film or playing games on the computer, but instead you are in this room and willing to face whatever adversity today brings. What I know about you is that you already have a high level of mental strength—or else you would not have made it this far. What I do not know is what the small fears and anxieties are that sometimes get in your way. Perhaps I could help you become a better player by helping you remove such anxieties and replace them with added confidence and belief. I look forward to working with you.

Coaches face similar challenges with their teams. In his final season as manager of Manchester United, Sir Alex Ferguson completed 3,000 competitive games with a win–loss record of almost 6 out of 10. The development of a successful team is interspersed with setbacks, defeats and failures. In the most competitive leagues even the greatest coaches and teams walk away from 4 or more games out of 10 having been defeated. Dealing with adversity is part of the fabric of competitive team sports.

Any game is winnable or losable; the bounce of the ball, referee's decisions or injuries can influence passages of play or even a result. The ability to absorb adversity and bounce back, perhaps best defined as resilience, is a mental skill that coaches can build in their players as part of the recipe for team success. In fact, this chapter could be turned to a positive tone by changing the title to 'Building Resilience'. This mindset skill is particularly important for modern young players who may not have faced any significant adversity in other areas of their life.

Understanding Adversity

Adversity is defined as a condition of misfortune or calamity, or a difficult or unpleasant event or circumstance. The nature of competitive soccer over a long league season means that teams will find it hard to avoid adverse situations such as these:

- Inconsistent form
- Loss of morale
- A failing coach
- Too much change
- Conflict
- Critical injuries
- Loss of team discipline
- Critical incidents
- A talented but difficult star player.

The effect of adversity is first felt in the collective mindset of the team when their normally controlled and positive mindset (see figure 13.1a) becomes uncontrolled and heads in a negative direction (see figure 13.1b). The unprepared team abandon disciplined thinking and react emotionally to the negative feelings, including the frustration and helplessness that often accompany adversity. Essentially, such a team move from fighter mentality to victim mentality, feel overwhelmed by the crisis and become unable to deal with the problem or find a way to move forward. Younger teams may also suffer a shock to their identity, realising that they are not perfect and feeling the guilt of letting down themselves, their club, family and friends.

Here is a simple example of the way in which a team have learned to deal with an adverse game situation and retain a composed, positive mindset, as in figure 13.1a:

> You may encounter defeats but you must not be defeated. In fact, it may be necessary to encounter the defeats, so you can know who you are, what you can rise from, and how you can still overcome.
>
> Maya Angelou
> Poet, actor and civil rights activist

- Adversity strikes (e.g., the goalkeeper fails to save an easy shot).
- The player calmly thinks through her or his response (I need to forget that mistake and stay in this game).
- The decision is accompanied by a positive emotion (I still believe in myself).
- The goalkeeper moves on to the next situation (signals to teammates that she or he has recovered).

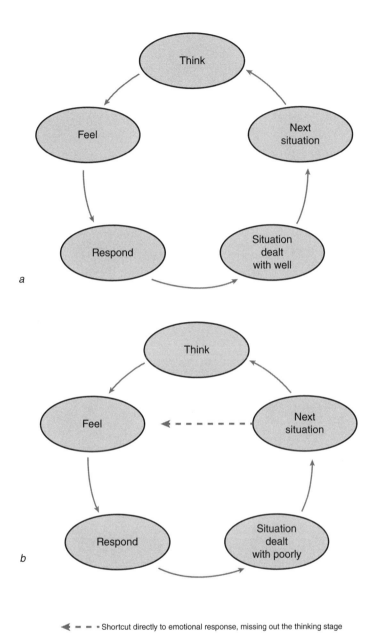

FIGURE 13.1 *(a)* Staying in control when dealing with adverse game situations; *(b)* becoming out of control when reacting to adverse game situations.

Coaches train their players and team to think clearly and calmly when dealing with fast and ever-changing game scenarios. This approach gives the team a mechanism that helps overcome adverse game situations and allows the players to move on while retaining a positive mindset.

Figure 13.1*b* illustrates how a team have failed to retain a composed, positive mindset when dealing with an adverse game situation. The players take an emotional shortcut and go straight to how they feel (OMG!), skipping the crucial thinking phase. The emotion is likely to be negative—anger, fear or guilt. This knee-jerk response will quite possibly lead to an even worse next situation. So in the previous example, the goalkeeper does not think through the mistake. The keeper overacts emotionally, loses belief and focus, is in a worse position to deal with the next situation and may lose the confidence of his or her teammates.

Reacting emotionally to a series of adverse situations, rather than learning to deal with them, can cause any individual or team, in life, business or sport, to decline, as described by Rosabeth Moss Kanter (2004) in her book *Confidence*:

> Of all the pathologies that accumulate in a losing streak, one of the most damaging to individuals, and eventually to the places they work and live, is passivity and learned helplessness. When people become resigned to their fate, nothing ever changes.
>
> Self-direction is supposedly a basic human desire, but under some circumstances it can wither with neglect.
>
> People who find themselves in losing situations are
>
> - more easily fatigued,
> - more often injured and
> - call in sick more often.
>
> When people are surrounded by pessimism—that feeling that they are victims of uncontrollable forces around them—they drag others down with them, finding the worst in everything, or resisting other people's ideas but offering none of their own. With diminished initiative, innovation disappears, problems go unsolved, opportunities go unseized. The cycle gets harder to break.

The mental strength of a team begins with the recognition that adversity is part of the challenge of competitive sport. A characteristic of teams with a championship mindset is they are better prepared to handle adversity than their opponents. They have built sufficient resilience to overcome problems. A healthy and strong team mindset does not suffer significant damage when setbacks occur.

Dealing With Downward Spirals

During a long, competitive league season, teams can be on an upward spiral, experiencing good achievement and momentum; they can be on

A goalie needs mental toughness to not sink into a negative mindset when a goal is conceded.

a plateau, seeing little progress or decline; or they can be in a downward spiral, dealing with an accumulation of negative thoughts, feelings and actions that bottoms out as a slump.

When adversity strikes, pressure goes up, whether real or perceived, and it becomes easier to be pessimistic and drawn into a negative mindset. Coaches must not allow adversity to become the starting point for a downward spiral.

In my experience the playing season demands attention on so much day-to-day detail that managers and coaches in a soccer club often do not have the space or time to reflect on the big picture. This lack of perspective can mean that the effect of adversity is not recognised soon enough, so an insidious descent into a downward spiral begins to gather pace. Upward spirals need recognising and encouraging, often by doing less rather than more, whereas downward spirals need awareness and remedial action as early as possible.

> Decline generally does not stem from a single factor, but from an accumulation of decisions, actions and commitments that become entangled in a self-perpetuating system of dynamics. Once a cycle of decline is established it's hard to simply call a halt, put on the brakes, and reverse direction. The system has momentum. Expectations have formed, and they can turn into a culture that perpetuates losing.
>
> Rosabeth Moss Kanter (2004)

TABLE 13.1 **Downward Spirals**

Signs	Coach action
Warning signs are ignored.	Constantly aware and vigilant.
Defensiveness and denial increase.	Stay open-minded and check information.
Communication decreases.	Create communication and keep no secrets.
Confidence crumbles.	
Only answer seems to be to work harder.	Refocus on team strengths and successes.
Criticism and blaming increase.	No punishment, work smarter.
Isolation increases, and 'silos' are created.	Remind everyone of personal responsibilities.
Focus turns inward.	
'We' culture becomes 'me' culture.	Inject social activity and togetherness.
Initiative decreases.	Stop team from beating themselves up.
Aspirations diminish.	Ask seniors for more team leadership.
Coaches grasp for quick fixes.	Challenge players to step up.
Negativity spreads.	Agree on new goals for the season.
Panic and haste	Counsel patience and staying power.
Team feel helpless and stop trying.	Change the story and emphasise the positive.
Team capitulate, give up.	Don't allow setbacks to affect composure.
	Take the lead in fighting on.
	Have a clear-the-air meeting and create action plan to recover.

Coaches must learn to read the increasingly damaging signals (see table 13.1) and take immediate steps to halt and then reverse the spiral, building resilience for future situations.

Creating a Blueprint for Recovery From Adversity

Schinke et al. (2004), in a research paper on teaching resilience, identify that handling adversity starts in the mind of the athlete. Depending on their level of optimism ('I can do this') or pessimism ('This is beyond me'), athletes interpret their performance in different ways. Optimistic, positive athletes explain a performance in terms of controllable factors, accepting responsibility and accountability and therefore staying in control. The more pessimistic athletes seize on uncontrollable factors, such as rotten weather, bad refereeing or a poor away playing surface, to protect their egos. They do not accept responsibility or accountability and lose control over any process of learning or bouncing back. They suffer what Seligman (1998) called 'learned helplessness'.

When asked to help soccer teams deal with adversity, I follow a practical three-stage process:

1. Help the coaches and team reframe the situation from threat to challenge.
2. Deal with the accompanying negative emotions, frustration and sense of helplessness by changing the story from negative back to positive.
3. Develop an appropriate coping strategy that coaches and players agree to follow to regain improved performance.

Within this process the following sequence of steps helps create forward impetus:

- **Establish the context**. Confirm exactly what the situation is. Help coaches and the team rise above their immediate situation and see the bigger picture, the overall context. Look for positive points. Nail down the key problems and barriers to performance. Separate controllables from uncontrollables.

- **Increase communication**. Defuse the situation with increased communication. Share issues, thus reducing anxiety and emotion. Reengage everyone in the dialogue that will begin to produce shared solutions.

- **Restate (or reframe) team goals**. Be clear on what the expectations are and ask what is now reasonable to expect given the circumstances. Stop looking backwards ('What has happened?'). Build realistic optimism by agreeing new, achievable team objectives on which to refocus.

- **Reevaluate resources**. Can recovery happen and can goals be met by the present group of players and coaches? When adversity is prolonged and helplessness has set in, then significant change and reinvention has to be considered. The most effective solution may be a change of coach or fresh talent to bring renewed optimism, energy and enthusiasm.

Persistence Is the Key to Beating Adversity

Persistence is always trying.
Persistence is never quitting.
Persistence means giving your best.
Persistence means being positive.
Persistence means being productive.
Persistence means keeping believing.
Persistence means staying in the game.
Persistence means trying one more time.
Persistence overcomes resistance.
Persistence pays in the end.

- **Investigate the options**. How can positive change be achieved? What choices are available? What must be done, should be done, might be done and must not be done? All ideas should be considered. This process should be shared. Very often the best answers come from the players themselves, especially the seniors.

- **Relate consequences to options**. Consider each option and check the range of potential consequences. Eliminate those options where the consequences are unacceptable.

- **Decide on the solution**. After the right option is decided upon, do not compromise on the best solution for recovery—there may be no gain without pain! If possible the recovery plan should be acceptable to, and shared by, both coaches and players. Breaking down a complex solution into parts and presenting it one step at a time is sometimes more palatable and appropriate.

- **Agree on an action plan**. Create a step-by-step action plan. Aim for some early successes and celebrate them. These signs of progress will fuel optimism and build confidence in the direction of travel. Renewed energy allows everyone to redouble her or his efforts, led by the coach.

- **Change the story**. Replace the present story of the team and their pessimistic, negative mindset with a new story of optimism and hope to rebuild energy and enthusiasm. The players must hear the new story confirmed from the club, the coaches and the significant adults around them. The story must excite and confirm the way forward to the players. This is a time when trust in the coach and the team leaders is most tested.

- **Hold your nerve**. Change takes time, and sometimes it's two steps forward, one step back. Leaders must hold their nerve, stick to the script agreed and continue to show supportive, calm patience.

Coach Bill Walsh (2009, p 12) establishes five don'ts while this process is taking place.

1. Don't ask, 'Why me?'

2. Don't expect sympathy.

3. Don't bellyache.

4. Don't keep accepting condolences.

5. Don't blame others.

Dealing With a Thunderbolt

This term is used to describe those games, normally a couple every season, when you confidently expect your team to play well and win and the opposite happens.

- Avoid any initial emotional overreaction.
- Accept that thunderbolts happen to all teams.
- Get the evidence right.
- Start with what worked.
- Start with who worked.
- Identify what didn't work (one off or not).
- Identify who didn't work (can't or won't).
- What or who must change?
- What or who must not change?
- How are changes to be made?
- What is the time scale?
- What happens if nothing is done?

Building Resilience

Change is an inevitable consequence in competitive soccer as the game and each team evolve. Through experience, the great coaches see change coming early, find flexible ways to deal with it, sell the benefits to the team and move on quickly. They find ways to manage transition without destroying the positive mindset of the team. These coaches have built personal resilience, the mental capacity to deal with and recover from adverse situations and can teach their teams the same mental skill. The coach's resilience has been tested in many situations, such as the following examples:

- Steve McClaren arrived at Derby County FC midseason and changed from a 4-4-2 system to a 4-3-3 possession ball game.
- Brendan Rogers 'modernised' Liverpool FC by changing tactics and attitudes and playing to win rather than not to lose.
- Mike Noonan, the men's soccer head coach at Clemson University, replaced a failed culture with a high-value achievement culture, on and off the field. His persistence in developing the right conditions paid off with the 2014 ACC Championship.

What these coaches have in common is the ability to hold their nerve under pressure and see the change through without damaging the mind-set of their teams.

Shelley and Jamie Smith, the coaches of the University South Carolina (USC) women's soccer team, have faced more than their fair share of adversity in building their 2014 ACC Championship team. The key words they use constantly are team, family and grit. Strength in adversity has been defined as grit (Seligman 2011)—a combination of passion and toughness. Seligman, drawing on the research of Angela Duckworth, relates achievement to both skill and effort. Those with modest skills can still achieve with great effort—the grit of passion and toughness.

> The real leverage you have for more achievement is more effort. Effort is no more and no less than how much time you practise on the task. Time on task acts in two ways to increase achievement: it multiplies existing skill and knowledge, and it also directly increases skill and knowledge. The best news is that effort is very malleable. How much time you devote to the task comes from the exercise of conscious choice—from free will. Choosing to devote time to an endeavour comes from at least two aspects of positive character: self-control and *grit*. (Seligman 2011, p 125)

Dealing with adversity for USC women's soccer means showing the unselfishness of a team, the closeness of a family and the grit to respond to tough times. They have the passion to turn up ready to play every day, win or lose, and the toughness to persist when times are difficult.

Coach Smith builds such resilience in her team by simulating likely adverse situations and asking the question, 'If this happened then what would be your response?' This probing helps the team

- understand what can get in the way,
- identify the most likely obstacles,
- decide how they might deal with them together,
- consider how they will react when things don't go as planned and
- build the role of team leaders and seniors.

Such what-if exercises develop a mental toughness that views adversity as a challenge

> There are a lot of variables in my season. Injuries, the schedule, a losing streak, whatever. And you can't predict those things. But of all those things, the one element that no one from the outside knows about is what goes on in the locker-room, the dynamic of how 53 different guys interact, who the 'go-to' guys are. The more of those guys you have, the better chance you have of being successful.
>
> Tiki Barber
> New York Giants running back

and an opportunity to reinforce a team with esteem and toughness and build resilience. This approach is how coaches teach mental toughness. Teams become what they think about most.

I recently advised an international team going on a foreign tour. The games were of less concern than the general conditions to be faced. Having spoken to the coaches, team and especially the charismatic captain, we decided on a catchphrase to symbolise our resilient approach to adversity. When the bus taking the team from the airport to their hotel broke down, the captain stood up, looked down the bus and calmly but strongly said, 'Just deal with it!' The team handled that and a number of other setbacks with resilience (and good humour!). This response carried over to success on the field.

Another exercise that helps teams overcome adversity is based on raising the belief of the team in themselves and each other. The coaches start by expressing their belief in the team. They then set up the team for a later meeting when each player will be asked to say three positive things about a teammate (the name to be texted to each player by the coach the day before). This exercise can have a powerful effect, especially as a big-game boost. Players are given permission to say things they normally wouldn't, and they also hear some positive things about themselves.

Coaches as Role Models

When adversity strikes a team, all eyes turn to the coach. No matter how the coach is feeling personally, he or she is now the public face of the team, and his or her appearance, body language, words and actions are vital in the process of recovery from adversity. When conducting a mental health check on teams, I always begin with the coaches and check that they are directing their power and authority in optimistic, positive and productive ways, reflecting challenge and not threat. I check whether the head coach and the coaching staff are doing the following:

- Looking good
- Smiling and communicating
- Being busy and energetic
- Carrying out a plan of action and being purposeful
- Being realistic but optimistic
- Neither blaming nor accepting excuses
- Using their hard-gained knowledge and experience
- Emphasising the positive
- Keeping everything in perspective

To achieve such a positive mindset, coaches must be able to view an adverse situation in a particular way: (1) temporary as against ongoing, (2) localized as against all encompassing and (3) correctable as against unchangeable.

Coaches are constantly shaping their team's mindset, especially post-game when a team can be coming off a win with a good performance, a win after a poor performance, a defeat despite a good performance or a defeat after a poor performance.

The coach must communicate the right message in an honest appraisal, directing the team how to feel, indicating accountability but without blame, identifying what lessons can be learned and concluding by giving hope for the future.

Senior players can also be role models. The benefit of their experience is that adversity will be familiar. They have the knowledge that tough times don't last but tough players do, and they have built the resilience needed to cope with adversity.

Great Poster in a Locker-Room

Get turned on by difficulty.
Get psyched up by problems.
Get excited by obstacles.

The challenge of competition means that all soccer players, teams and coaches will face adversity from time to time. This must be accepted as part of the journey and coached like any other challenge. The eventual winners will be separated from the losers by a number of factors, but one of the most important is the development of mental strength to cope with the adverse moments of any season.

BEATING THE SLUMP

Coach Mark sought help when his team had lost six games in a row and were firmly locked at the bottom of their league. As coach of a professional team, he knew that such a downward spiral was serious.

Our initial conversation was designed to bring the coach himself back to a positive frame of mind. I stressed several points:

- Every team will have a difficult period.
- There is enough time to recover the situation.
- The only answer is you, work and persistence.
- See this as a challenge, not a threat.
- This period will define you, the coaches and the players, as men, not just professionals.
- When this slump is over, you will all be in a better place and mentally tougher.

After Mark was on board and back into realistic optimism, we moved on to agree on a coping strategy.

1. Remove the fear and make soccer enjoyable again.
2. Change the story and therefore attitudes—the glass is always half full:
   - Remind the team of past successes.
   - Emphasise that they are a good team in a bad phase.
   - Remind them that much of their game is still good.
   - Change the conversations from negative to positive.
3. Take control:
   - Don't look outside for a culprit—no blaming.
   - Avoid comparison with others—the fight is with ourselves.
   - Emphasise that the team are not powerless and that they control their own destiny.
   - Let go of the past and live in the present.
4. Focus:
   - What can't we control?
   - What can we control?
   - What are the priorities?

5. Change—restructure progress:
   - Make a fresh start.
   - Set a new work pattern.
   - Create a new self-image.
6. Recovery:
   - Set small targets as steppingstones on the journey.
   - Celebrate each forward step achieved and rebuild good feelings.
7. Expect and deal with setbacks on the way to recovery.
8. Believe in the process, expect success and develop positive team images.

Slowly, the team found a more positive attitude and renewed energy, and the turnaround began. Mark was back to his enthusiastic self and led the team to a more positive and stronger mentality. They did not suddenly become a great team, but they did improve enough to avoid relegation.

Chapter 14

KEEPING FRESH

When FC Twente was on the way to winning their first Dutch Eredivisie title, they faltered with six games to go. The then assistant coach, Alfred Schreuder, described it as a collective loss of spirit, enjoyment and energy. In a meeting, the coaching staff decided that the long, pressurized season, especially the burden of being top of the league and being chased rather than chasing, had finally caught up with the team. Players were withdrawing, becoming passive and oversensitive and suddenly looking tired of each other. They had lost their freshness.

During the discussion I reminded the coaches of the four freshness killers of teams and players by writing the word *HATE* on the board:

H = hunger

A = anger

T = tiredness

E = emotion

Any of the four can destroy performance.

The coaches recognised that tiredness and emotion were the problems in this situation, and they needed to freshen things up. Suggestions included changing practice, rotating players, team meetings, top-up fitness sessions, social trips and so on. What was eventually decided, despite great reservation expressed by the coaches, was to give everybody a complete two-day break from the soccer club.

The result was dramatic. Staff and players returned with energy and excitement. They were looking forward to seeing each other and were ready to go. The team went on to win their first-ever league title. Sometimes in soccer less is more!

Managing Team Freshness

Good coaches manage a game. Great coaches manage a season. Many times during a long competitive league season, a surprising result occurs and the losing coach will say that his or her team were just not ready to play. The challenge to coaches is to keep the team fresh—physically, mentally and emotionally—so that they are always ready and have the energy and willpower to compete. The demands of soccer are such that managing team freshness and energy can be the difference between a winning and losing season.

In this situation the passion and intensity of the coaches can get in the way. In all my mentoring scenarios with coaches at all levels, the one thing I have found most difficult to get across is the importance of balancing work with recovery and monitoring and maintaining team freshness. For coaches, and I understand this conviction, there is never enough time with the team to teach the techniques and tactics of soccer. As a result they try to teach too much and work too hard and long, both confusing and tiring the players. The effects obviously become more harmful as the season goes on. As players lose freshness, they begin to stop learning or giving 100 per cent effort. As the great American football coach Vince Lombardi said, 'Fatigue makes cowards of us all'.

I always urge coaches to work from the game backwards. I ask the key question, 'What state would you like your team to be in on game day?' The answer is always, 'Fresh, energetic and ready to compete for 90 (plus) minutes'. Yet the same coaches often overcoach and overtrain their teams during the week and take their game legs away. Although coaches must challenge their teams with the hard work of preparation, they must also recognise when enthusiasm and focus dip. At this point keeping the team fresh is the coach's top priority. Rest is as important as work.

Performance readiness, often summarised by coaches as freshness, is recognisable when a team are physically, mentally and emotionally prepared:

- Switched on—alert, aware, engaged
- Confident and optimistic
- Highly energised
- Focused and in the present

Leaders Keep Their Teams Fresh

The art of leadership requires knowing when it makes sense to take people over the top, to push them to their highest level of effort, and when to take your foot off the accelerator a little. If your team is constantly working on adrenalin, in a crisis mode, running as hard as they can, they become vulnerable. When an emergency arises, when the competition suddenly presents an unexpected threat, your team has no next level to step up to, no reserves to draw on.

The best leaders are those who understand the levels of energy and focus available within their team. They also recognise which situations require extreme effort and which do not. Knowing the difference ensures that your organisation is fresh and fully able to perform at its uppermost levels when it's necessary.

Bill Walsh (2009)

Managing individual and team performance readiness and keeping everybody fresh (including the staff) are critical to allowing talent and skill to flourish. Without a careful balance of work, rest and

> Managing energy, not time, is the key to high performance, health and happiness.
>
> Jim Loehr and Tony Schwarz (2003)

recovery, what appear to be technical, tactical or mental performance problems could simply be fatigue. The story about FC Twente at the start of this chapter was simply that the team had been running on empty.

Freshness and Team Mindset

Jim Loehr and Tony Schwarz (2003), in an examination of toughness training, emphasised the view that athletes are compromised if they don't have the right quantity, quality, focus and force of energy to manage the challenge to be faced.

The higher the level of competition is, the greater the need is for the players to be fresh and have a full tank of energy. Coaches who are serious about performing well every game should treat the season as a series of sprints, not as a marathon (see figure 14.1), allowing the team to replenish energy between sprints and boost mental and emotional strength. This preparation allows the players to be fully engaged before the start of every game, whether it is the opening game or the last phase of the season.

Full recovery is essential for total reengagement (see figure 14.2). Without full recovery, the energy tank gradually drains, intensity dips, full engagement is not possible, and a defeat is more likely. Without a proper recovery that fully replaces energy expended, player performance will dip. Mentally, the team are more likely to be vulnerable to fatigue, poor decision making and loss of emotional control, causing frustration, anger and so on.

The link between energy and team mindset is strong. Mental toughness is defined as disciplined thinking and action under pressure and fatigue. Energy is the currency of sport, and fatigue can cause the strongest player or team to fail under pressure and in critical moments. Tables 14.1 and 14.2 demonstrate the links between attitude, emotion, energy and performance in relation to confidence and mental toughness.

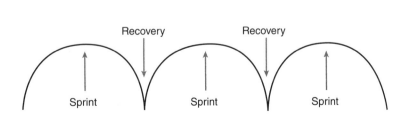

FIGURE 14.1   The season as a series of sprints and full recovery.

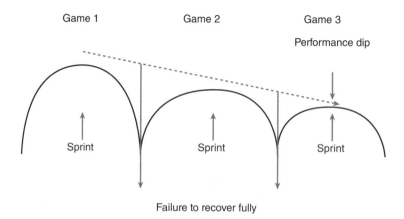

Game 1   Game 2   Game 3

Performance dip

Sprint   Sprint   Sprint

Failure to recover fully

FIGURE 14.2 Failure to recover fully leads to performance dips.

TABLE 14.1 Relationship Between Confidence and Energy

	Player A	Player B
Attitude	Confident	Lacking confidence
Emotions	Excited, vigorous	Anxious, frustrated
Energy	Positive, high	Negative, low
Performance outcome	Successful	Unsuccessful

TABLE 14.2 Mentally Tough Versus Mentally Weak Striker After Missing a Goal

	Mentally tough	Mentally weak
Attitude change	Thinks, 'I'll get the next one!' Remains positive and does not lose self-belief.	Thinks, 'I'll never score now!' Becomes negative and loses all self-belief.
Emotional response	Remains enthusiastic, stimulated and optimistic.	Becomes irritated and discouraged, loses hope and may blame others.
Resultant energy state	Remains positive in direction and high in intensity.	Becomes negative in direction and low in intensity.
Effect on performance	More likely to recover well and score with a later chance.	Becomes increasingly passive, hides, is more concerned with not missing again than working for another chance to score.

States and Sources of Energy

Energy can be characterised in four ways:

- Positive and high—'I am really passionate about this game'.
- Positive and low—'I am relaxed about this game'.
- Negative and high—'I am fearful and tense about this game'.
- Negative and low—'We have no chance today'.

Peak performance is possible only when a team feel fresh. Figure 14.3 illustrates the link between the energy state and the mindset of a team. A team who arrive at the game with high, positive energy, the top left-hand sector, are more likely to win. Fuelled by their energy and freshness, they have the following competitive mindset:

- They have defined the situation positively—'We can win today'.
- They are fully engaged—'We are fully committed to the challenges ahead'.
- They are driven to win—'We have prepared well, feel ready and deserve to win'.
- They are relaxed yet ready—'This should be fun today!'

Coaches now have a clear guideline on how to prepare their team with a combination of work and proper recovery leading to the optimum game mindset. Of course, the opposite is also true. When coaches over-coach and overtrain their team—all work and pressure and insufficient

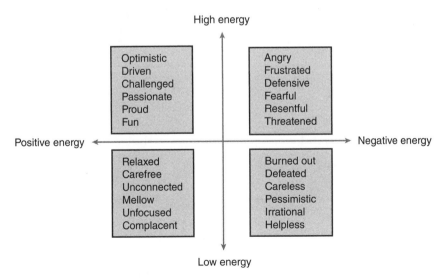

FIGURE 14.3 Energy states.

Adapted from J. Loehr and T. Schwartz, 2003, *On form* (London: Nicholas Brealey), 10.

rest and recovery—the team can begin games in the energy state and mindset described as low and negative in the bottom right-hand corner. Depleted of energy and freshness, players may face a game with the following mindset:

- They define the situation negatively—'We can't win today'.
- They are not engaged—'We are not fully committed to this game'.
- They lack focus and intensity—'We are too tired to concentrate'.
- They are tense—'We feel helpless and can't enjoy the moment'.

During the course of a long competitive season, teams may sway between high positive energy and low negative energy. Coaches and their support staff must be vigilant and recognise early any changes in energy state and be mindful of the likely impact on team mindset.

Table 14.3 offers coaching staff a quick assessment of their team's readiness to play. Coaches should answer these questions independently and then share their answers. Any answer that is not scored high should make the coaches reflect on their preparation leading up to the game and on whether they have failed to maintain freshness and energy.

In a soccer context, coaches have access to five sources of energy with which to fuel their teams.

TABLE 14.3 Questions for Coaches: Determining Team Readiness to Play

Pregame observations	High (✓)	Average (✓)	Low (✓)
1. Do the team look happy to be playing?			
2. Are they excited?			
3. Do they welcome the challenge?			
4. Are they determined?			
5. Are the leaders leading?			
6. Is there energy in the locker-room?			
7. Are they confident of success?			
8. Are they focused on the positive?			
9. Are the team together?			
10. Are they in their pregame routines?			
Total (✓)	Ready	Unsure	Not ready

1. Physical—energy that the body needs to function at the level required, obtained through exercise, nutrition, hydration, sleep, rest, recovery.
2. Mental—energy needed to perform mental tasks, obtained through optimism, purpose, direction, belief and positive talk.
3. Emotional—emotional connections that can be made to the challenge, obtained through team identity, motivational talks, camaraderie, fun.
4. Spiritual—energy gained from pursuing goals, having faith or upholding values, obtained through a strong sense of purpose or belief.
5. Social—social relationships gained from interacting with others, obtained through team harmony, bonding, effective player leadership, stability.

If a team lose freshness and experience a physical or mental dip, coaches can check through these five sources of energy and seek ways to nourish their team with new supplies. A coaching philosophy that embraces an awareness of the everyday needs of players gives a coach the best opportunity to maintain team freshness throughout the season. Keeping the team topped up with high, positive energy is essential to optimising engagement and performance.

Managing Energy

Major national or international soccer competitions usually fall at the end of a demanding competitive domestic or conference league season. In these situations the coach of the representative team has the task of welding high-performing club players into a cohesive force in limited preparation time, refreshing elite players after a long season and then maintaining the team's high, positive energy through a tournament, often over several weeks in a new, perhaps unfamiliar, environment.

The World Cup is the highest profile example. When England competed in the 2010 competition, held in South Africa, the team had a five-week preparation period in a remote ranch. Although this environment allowed good physical preparation, it did not nourish the team mentally, emotionally or socially. This circumstance contributed significantly to the resultant underachievement of the team. England were on an early flight home.

When a team are physically, mentally and emotionally fresh, they are always more likely to be optimistic and excited about new challenges.

Staying fresh and building and maintaining energy means understanding what gives energy and what takes it away.

Energy givers include these factors:

- Purpose and goals
- Proper preparation
- Clarity of individual roles
- Clarity of team game plan
- Home games
- Inspirational leadership
- Previous good results
- Pride in the shirt
- Positive rituals
- Love of the challenge
- Fun, enjoyment, variety
- Team cohesion

Energy drainers include these factors:

- Overtraining
- Overcoaching
- Lack of continuity and stability
- Repetition leading to boredom
- Poor leadership
- Unrealistic expectations
- Distractions and lifestyle issues
- Negative people
- Anxiety and fear
- Team conflict
- A blame culture
- Lack of enjoyment and boredom

Energy renewal and retaining team freshness are more than the absence of work. Every player needs to adopt good habits and be in a supportive coaching environment that takes care of both body and mind, encompassing a range of factors, such as the following:

- Sleep
- Active and passive rest
- Relaxation exercises

- Meditation and yoga
- Healthy eating
- Closing down games in a positive manner
- Good communication to decrease anxiety
- Personal feedback
- Counselling if needed
- Change of environment
- Positive people and emotional nourishment

Player's Guide to Keeping Fresh

Invest in your energy levels.
Train to build greater energy capacity.
Treat recovery and downtime seriously.
Take care of your general health.
Eat well and regularly and keep fully
    hydrated.
Maintain consistent sleep patterns.
Seek out energy fillers.
Avoid energy drainers.
Don't let problems fester.
Develop positive energy rituals.
Find relaxing interests outside soccer.
Maximise every recovery opportunity.

When good energy management does not take place, player burnout can occur. Players can simply lose interest in playing, and it becomes a job, not a joy. For teams in tough, competitive league situations, the energy demanded often exceeds the supply available. The lack of adequate recovery time combined with emotional exhaustion can create burnout conditions for both players and coaches.

Many interrelated variables act together to cause player or team burnout. Several factors commonly contribute to burnout:

- Demanding practice conditions in terms of frequency and intensity
- Unrealistic expectations
- Confused, inconsistent or harsh behaviour of the coaches
- Extreme physical fatigue
- Lack of care caused by poor communication and feedback from coaches
- Inadequate or inappropriate social support group

The personality and style of the coach can act as either a buffer against or a catalyst for player or team burnout.

Coaches also have a responsibility to maintain their own freshness and energy levels and thus avoid personal burnout. This situation results from a building up of stress over time and causes the coach to experience mental, emotional and physical exhaustion. Consequences can include negative self-concept, poor attitudes to work, life and other people and loss of idealism, energy and purpose. Coaches should follow the freshness guidelines they set for their teams by managing their time effectively. The critical elements are work-recovery balance, relaxation, exercise, variety and a clear focus in dealing with controllable factors.

Monitoring Team Freshness

I was once present at what appeared to be a near-perfect practice. The practice was on Thursday, and the big game was two days later on Saturday. The head coach understood that the team had built up great energy and emotional power after Thursday's work. The issue was how to maintain optimum freshness. The decision was made to have a short 45-minute practice on Friday. It would be quick, sharp and fun, maintaining the team's high, positive energy and emotional state (the top left-hand sector of figure 14.3).

All was well until a senior coach intervened and asked for more practice time on Friday. Under pressure the head coach relented and agreed. That's when the problems began. On the way to practice the weather changed for the worse, and the players were met with wet, cold conditions. Then the 45-minute practice became a 75-minute practice, and many players stood about for the final 30 minutes.

I watched as the positive, high energy created on Thursday changed to low, negative energy (the bottom right-hand sector of figure 14.3). A strong emotional conviction about winning the game weakened. Players who knew on Thursday that they were ready were confused on Friday by the need for extra practice and an overload of information.

Overtraining, overcoaching and mental and emotional confusion led to a poor performance—an own goal before the game had begun. The coaches got in the way of the team performance. Changes in attitude can be observed from changes in player behaviour. Table 14.4 indicates some of the changes that should alert coaches to the dangers of overtraining or overcoaching.

TABLE 14.4   Attitude Killers From Overtraining and Overcoaching

Physical	Mental	Emotional
Fatigue	Confused thinking	Boredom
Muscle soreness	Poor concentration	Lack of enjoyment
Injuries	Persistent mistakes	Depression
Illness	Mental fatigue	Sadness
Aches and pains	Irrational thinking	Low motivation
Eating problems	Negative thinking	Anger and moodiness
Strength problems		Anxiety
Weight problems		

Coaches monitor their team's freshness, energy and emotional levels by following these pointers within their planned programme.

1. Setting an Example

In physics, the definition of power is the rate at which work is done or energy is transferred. The most powerful coaches transmit a positive energy that fuels their team. Energy is infectious, so the coach must be a model of good energy. The coaching style and messages must give energy, be optimistic, confident and motivational and not take energy away by being pessimistic and demoralizing.

2. Inspiring With Ideas

Achievement requires energy, and energy comes from emotion. Emotion is released by ideas, and ideas come from coaches, through optimistic, positive and inspirational messages. For example, planning and programming a short motivational team meeting can be a way of quickly reenergising the team. This has to be used sparingly and not become a routine activity.

3. Dealing With Defeat and Setbacks

By staying optimistic, by educating rather than blaming and by interpreting a defeat or a setback calmly and positively, the coach is demonstrating role model behaviour that assists in building the emotional intelligence of the team. Pessimism and blame have a negative effect on team freshness.

4. Adjusting to Special Circumstances

Planning to keep a team fresh throughout a season is based on the foreseen, likely programme of games. But the programme may change unexpectedly—an extended cup run, playoffs at the end of the season, a surprise invitation to a tournament and so on. To stay fresh despite these possible late additions, coaches should think creatively.

- They can plan for their possible inclusion. (Coach Belichick of the New England Patriots always organises his programme of work from the Super Bowl backwards.)
- They can build a squad who can deal with the extra challenges.
- They should create a can-do mindset in the team—a team that can play anytime, anywhere, in any conditions.
- They can reschedule work, rest, recovery and relaxation to meet the special circumstances.

A COACH'S PROGRAMME TO STAY FRESH FOR PLAYOFFS

The benefit of keeping the team fresh is finishing the season (when the most important games are likely to be played) strong in body and mind. Strategies taken to manage energy and stay fresh during the course of the season can bring real rewards at the end. This point is especially true in leagues that end in playoffs.

Coach Jeff, a US college coach, sought my advice on getting his team in the best possible condition. He needed them fresh to be competitive in the playoffs. We discussed and agreed that the main dangers at playoff time would be physical fatigue and loss of mental strength and emotional control; little would change technically or tactically. The programme we devised had two elements—dealing with the emotions and building strategies to help keep the team as fresh as possible.

1. Set the Playoff Mindset by Ensuring Mental and Emotional Strength

- Calm the team down—it's just another step in the process of building the sustained success of this team.
- Remind the team how much they have improved and emphasise how well prepared they are.
- Show highlights of the season—the team deserve to be in the playoffs.
- Take control—'We define the situation; we shape our destiny'.
- Act bravely—this is an opportunity to succeed, not fail.
- Simulate the what-if scenarios.
- Describe the sideshow and agree not to get distracted.
- Beware of dreaming—focus on the now.
- Accept but ignore the expectations of others—'We concentrate on getting the job done'.
- Remove the fear—'What's the worst that can happen?'
- Talk about having fun in the playoffs.
- Emphasise the importance of life harmony, of clearing the mind for soccer at this important stage of the season.

2. Introduce Coping Skills to Keep the Team Fresh

- Shorten practice time without losing intensity or conditioning.
- Work smarter, not harder.
- Cut down on any extra physical work, weight training and so on.
- Emphasise good nutrition and hydration.
- Stress the need for good rest and recovery.
- When possible, allow the team a day off away from soccer.
- Set team standards but keep an eye on individual special needs.
- Pay extra attention to game scenarios—holding a lead, penalty shoot-out and so on.
- Stay true to what got the team to the playoffs—if it ain't broke, don't fix it!
- Ask the experienced players for more leadership.

The programme also emphasised the influence that Jeff would have on the team as a model of optimism, belief and energy. The coach must not see the playoffs as the big stage but as a fitting culmination to the work of the whole season. The more confident and relaxed the coach is, the more confident and relaxed the team will be.

Finally, we discussed the likely signs that would show whether Jeff's team were ready or not. If the team were ready, he should see a controlled tension, a readiness, a team coming closer together, good levels of communication, strong focus and commitment but lots of humour.

A team who are not ready might seem complacent, easy going, more 'me' than 'we'. Some players might be withdrawing or trying too hard, and a general feeling of unease might be present.

The final point I made to Jeff was that these strategies did not guarantee success, but they would stop the team from getting in their own way. If he could keep the team as fresh as possible, mentally, emotionally and physically, then he was giving them the best chance to produce their best soccer at playoff time.

Chapter 15

REPEATING SUCCESS

On the first day of the new season following Manchester United's historic treble-winning 1998–99 year, one player reported back carrying a large plastic bag. With a smile he began to distribute baseball caps emblazoned 'Treble Champions'. Just then the manager, Sir Alex Ferguson, walked in. He saw what was happening, threw all the caps back into the bag and stuffed the bag straight into the bin.

'That was last season. Boys, you have achieved absolutely nothing so far this season!'

Sir Alex gave his team a chance of repeating success by refusing to allow any potentially weak mindset to gain hold in a team who dwell too long on their success. Along with other management principles described in his Harvard Business School interview soon after his 2013 retirement, his philosophy was always to move on and innovate or be overtaken. This is how Ferguson put it: 'The message is simple: We cannot sit still at this club' (Elberse and Ferguson 2013).

Bill Walsh (2009, p 144) agrees: 'Success Disease makes people begin to forego to different degrees the effort, focus, discipline, teaching, teamwork, learning and attention to detail that brought 'mastery' and its progeny, success. The hunger is diminished, even removed in some people'.

Achieving success is one thing, but staying successful is quite another. One of the ironies of competitive soccer is that success can bring as many problems as failure does.

If coaches identify and analyse what these new problems are in their team's performance after winning, they are likely to discover that their team

- have not changed much physically, though perhaps they are a little fatigued,
- have not changed technically at all and
- have not changed tactically, because they are playing the same way that brought success.

The change is mental and emotional, having to deal with the new challenge of coping with the pressures of winning, the increased expectations and attention that is part of the sideshow of success.

> There is no guarantee, no ultimate formula for success. However, a resolute and resourceful leader understands that there is a multitude of means to increase the *probability* of success. And that's what it all comes down to, namely, intelligently and relentlessly seeking solutions that will increase your chance of prevailing in the competitive environment.
>
> Bill Walsh (2009)

Coaches need to be aware of the mental and emotional changes that can affect a team who have just tasted success. Even while celebrating with his or her team, the thinking coach begins to ponder the process of adapting the team to build onwards for future success. The actual process of analysing the success—what worked, what didn't, what was down to chance—helps to reduce the danger of a drift to overconfidence and complacency. Undertaking this process with coaching colleagues, support staff and perhaps senior players, where appropriate, is key to the process. Repeating success relies on a sustained programme of everyday efforts to maintain and strengthen the champion team's mindset.

Winning Changes Mindsets

Winning can change coach, player and team mindset from the positive drive that brought success into a negative weakness that fails to sustain further achievement. After winning, new pressures emerge, whether real or perceived, that challenge the established mindset.

1. Expectations

After a winning season people around the team, many of whom are significant influences on the way that players think and feel, hold the team to a new, higher standard. The team are expected to win again and again (often unrealistically). A good example is the team who win a league championship and are promoted to a higher league. Fans, media and so on expect the team to deliver the same results. Many such teams, from recreational youth teams up to professional league teams, are crushed by the weight of unrealistic expectations, fail to deal with the defeats that ensue and often return to the comfort zone of their original league in the following season.

2. Consequences

When a team at the top of the league table lose, the loss can be perceived as far more dramatic than any previous defeats the team has suffered when positioned lower in the league. Of course, it is just a loss, but winners have to deal with the enhanced consequences, often intensified by the reactions of the people who have influence on team and player mindset. The fear of consequences when required to repeat success can cause a team to choke. Players' minds switch ahead and become infected

---

Complacency Destroys

In 2008 Chelsea suffered a surprise 3-1 Champions League defeat away to Roma. Captain John Terry identified his team's complacent mindset:

> We sort of strolled in, thinking we were better than them, when clearly we're not. What was disappointing was that we didn't fight. Even after we went one and then two down, we didn't show the fight and desire that's got us where we've been over the past few years.
>
> First and foremost, when you go to a place like Roma you need to fight and show more determination than them. If it comes to quality, then nine times out of ten we're better than most sides. We have to start with the desire to win. (Hughes 2008)

---

by the consequences of an unexpected defeat. Anxiety about the outcome begins to shape the actual performance. Concentration, composure and momentum are all lost as the team effectively defeat themselves.

3. Sideshow
Winners inevitably attract greater attention, sometimes accompanied by celebrity status and often intensified by media attention. Without control, this prominence can be a major distraction to the mindset needed to maintain success. Team sport offers many examples of one-off champions but far fewer repeat champions. When teams of these two types are compared and examined, one of the essential differences is that the teams able to manage the distractions of the sideshow are the teams that stay engaged in the daily task of continual improvement. These are the teams that are more likely to repeat success.

Of course, most teams in a league are more used to chasing than being chased, and they may be very inexperienced at dealing with sudden success. Inevitably, most coaches spend far more time and effort developing the mental strength of their teams to handle failure than they do dealing with success. The players may be quite unprepared for the pressures that sudden success can bring, including the feeling of being on trial and being expected to exhibit excellence on demand. Eventually, a team can feel that they are in a no-win situation. If they lose they are ostracized, and if they win the pressure increases. This situation may eventually erode team mindset and commitment. The dangers of success are clear:

- Loss of hunger and commitment
- Complacency caused by living off past reputation (see the Chelsea report)
- Exhaustion caused by lack of recovery time
- Believing the praise and publicity

Handling Success—Three Types of Player Mindset

1. Those who reach the top because they believe they can. They are in the best position to sustain success.
2. Those who are capable of success but have difficulty handling the sideshow. They will need a lot of help to stay on top.
3. Those who are simply content to be in the team. They will not contribute to repeating success.

If a coach cannot teach her or his team to handle and get past these issues, then the team will not be able to sustain and repeat their success. Rather, they will falter and return to a position in the league where the pressure drops to a comfortable level.

The options facing coaches with teams who achieve success are to do nothing, to reestablish and grow the existing team or to reinvent the team by introducing new players.

In this situation, a great deal depends upon the resources available for the coach in the context of the agreed vision for the team and the club.

Focusing on Excellence

Once I had the experience of being part of a team in which the assistant coach set an excellent standard of performance every day. He constantly emphasised the satisfaction and joy of playing excellent soccer and rarely talked results. The team were highly successful until the assistant coach was headhunted by a much bigger club. The head coach took over team preparation, and immediately the agenda and focus changed from excellence to results. Both the team and I realised that the head coach did not understand what had made them successful. He set them off on a downward spiral. Despite my intervention, the head coach was fixated by results and demanded success by any means.

One of the main threats to the team who find success through excellent performances is that they forget what got them there. Falling in love with success and the subsequent craving for winning results inevitably leads to less focus on the ongoing, continual process of building excellence. Table 15.1 shows the differences between focusing on success and focusing on excellence.

Focusing on excellence does not mean that a coach disregards the importance of winning soccer games. In fact, the opposite is true; coaches who take care of the process are more likely to benefit from the results.

Alfred Schreuder, now head coach of FC Twente in Holland, understands that at the highest level any game is winnable or losable. He wants his team to focus on both excellence and success, so he establishes a

TABLE 15.1   Focusing on Success or Excellence

Success	Excellence
Tricky to achieve or maintain	Dependable and builds consistency
Perishable at any time	Lasting and built on good habits
Difficult to control	Can be directed and controlled
Score fixated	Guided by a passion for quality
Can burden the team	Builds respect for the game
Often a major distraction	Defeats become learning moments
Each defeat becomes a disaster	Reduces fear of losing and setbacks
The pressure is exhausting	No obsession with the score
Players and coaches more liable to burn out	Players and coaches grow as people
Success of others is threatening	No resentment of others' success
Often exposes lack of emotional intelligence	Builds good emotional intelligence
'The pursuit of success makes a poor cornerstone for life'.	'The quality of a person's life is in direct proportion to the commitment to excellence'.

'winning zone' for his team to achieve. He does not ask them to be top of the league, a goal that heightens pressure and anxiety. He simply asks them to stay in the top six teams. A defeat does not become a disaster, and the team are not distracted from the focus on excellence. Later on in the season, if and when appropriate, Alfred adjusts the goal to top four and near the end of the season, to top two!

This is the advice I offered Alfred and the team when they found themselves leading the pack in the final phase of the season and there was a danger of losing focus:

- Stay true to what got you to the top.
- Talk excellence, not points.
- Focus on the now—beware of dreaming.
- Refuse to be distracted by the sideshow.
- Experienced players need to step up.
- Stay cool—a defeat is just a lost opportunity.
- Be brave—embrace and enjoy success.

If you believe you will be champions then you will practice like a number one team. If you practice like a number one team then you will play like a number one team. When you play like a number one team that's exactly where you will finish!

Tommy Lasorda
LA Dodgers baseball manager

Sustaining Excellence

Shortly after Sir Alex Ferguson acted to kill off overlong celebrations following Manchester United's treble-winning season, I was tasked with helping the team set goals for the new season. I was concerned about how we would set new goals after such an outstanding season. I shouldn't have worried! The team, led on this occasion by Gary Neville and Ryan Giggs, came up with a beautiful response: 'Win again! Win better! Win with class!' This was the mindset of champions determined to sustain success!

We have established that the major change in a team who first experience significant success is mental and emotional. The strong collective mindset that drove the team to victory is now besieged by the increased expectations, greater consequences of any defeat and the heightened sideshow described earlier. The team now find themselves being chased instead of doing the chasing. Without intervention by the coaches the team may start to get in their own way. Individuals flushed by success begin to push their own agendas ahead of that of the team. The team may then display reduced cohesion. Coaches must prevent the spread of negative influences on mindset by reinforcing the mental strength of the team if it falters.

Figure 15.1 suggests a programme of recalibration actions for coaches who want to train their team's mindset to deal with success on the way to sustained excellence.

- Celebrate—reinforce the good feelings that accompany the initial success.
- Move on—the coach defines the end of celebrations and commences team preparation for the next challenge.
- Set new goals—the refocusing process is helped by agreement on the new goals to be achieved.
- Reengage—the coach remotivates the players so that they are invigorated and again commit themselves to the hard work ahead. New players may be recruited to strengthen the team.
- Refocus— to win again, the team have to narrow down attention on the tasks ahead. No distractions!
- Smart preparation—repeating success is tough, so the coach finds ways to keep players on track with new challenges to meet the desired objectives.

The whole philosophy of chasing excellence and mastery in soccer is that it can never be attained. But the pursuit ensures that the team achieve the highest level of performance possible.

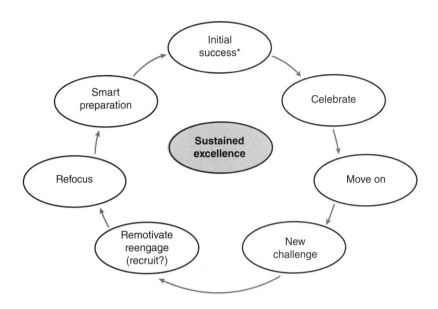

*The faster from success to moving on, the more time there
will be to concentrate on the new challenge ahead

FIGURE 15.1 The process of sustaining excellence.

Immediately after winning the Super Bowl, Coach Bill Belichick reverted to thinking of his team as number two.

He then went on to say, with all respect, that the team that had just won the Super Bowl had a lot of work to do to reach the ideal of consistent championship contenders. It meant that the team in the front office, coaches and scouts, were going to have to get back to work soon. And the team on the field shouldn't get too comfortable. He was asked how many players on the Super Bowl champs would have to be replaced before he could call them perennial championship threats. He didn't hesitate: 'About 20!' (Holley 2011, p 48)

**Coaches of Champion Teams
Who Repeat Success**

Have an insatiable passion for excellence

Employ the very best staff

Retain inspirational players

Have an intense belief in being the best

Build a history of success

Celebrate success and look beyond to greater things without delay

Never get tired of winning

Find key players to provide strong leadership

Adapt creatively to changing circumstances or increased competition

Plan for succession to stay ahead of the game

Coach's Checklist on Raising the Bar to Repeat Success

Questions that a coach must answer throughout the season.

	Yes	Somewhat	No
1. Have we improved our work ethic?			
2. Are the team as fit as they can be?			
3. Have we increased intensity and raised the level of internal competition?			
4. Have we raised quality by challenging players to be better?			
5. Have we given good enough feedback?			
6. Have we toughened responsibility and accountability?			
7. Have we set more complex training problems to make the team smarter?			
8. Do all the players understand the game plan?			
9. Do all the players understand their jobs?			
10. Can we be one of the best at set pieces?			
11. Have we identified players to be on or off the bus?			
12. Have we recruited well?			
13. Have we managed injury prevention well?			
14. Have we balanced stress and recovery?			
15. Are we ready to win again?			

Repeat champions who achieve ongoing excellence seem to have a number of enduring principles in common. In an excellent piece of research Yukelson and Rose (2014) determined 10 such principles:

1. Having a game plan to develop continuity and consistency from year to year.
2. Never playing to defend a title but rather to win a new one.
3. New and challenging goals especially emphasising performance excellence.
4. A daily dedication to practise with attitude and effort—'Today's preparation leads to tomorrow's performance'.
5. Attention to detail—an understanding that big games are won by moments of excellence.
6. Coaching for player accountability and self-responsibility.
7. Player leadership that releases the power of the locker-room.

8. Having team resiliency that ensures quick recovery from setbacks.

9. Quality relationships that reflect strong emotional ties between players.

10. Acceptance of team roles even when changed.

Finally, it helps if the coach, like Alfred Schreuder at FC Twente as described earlier, sets a team goal with some room to manoeuvre. Aiming solely for the number one spot can become self-defeating over time and may make attaining a second or third league place seem a failure. If the coach sets an early season goal of being in the top four, then there is wiggle room to maintain team belief in the case of one or two defeats. This approach is a great help to a team on the way to repeating success; players can endure a temporary dip without feeling like failures. At the appropriate time the coach can refine the team goal to being number one!

Guidelines for Players to Repeat Excellence

Be a fighter—never a victim.

Improve every day.

Think like a champion.

Preparation is everything.

Deal with the sideshow.

Beware celebrity.

Be a leader and step up.

Challenge yourself to be better.

Deal with the setbacks.

Think team—'we' not 'me'.

Stay in the race.

'If it is to be, it is up to me'.

Photo courtesy of FC Twente.

Setting new and realistic goals early each season gives players a chance to repeat success.

OVERCOMING THE PRESSURE OF SUCCESS

Coach Kerri e-mailed me about her successful U18 girls team:

We have averaged 13 wins a year and regularly qualify for the playoffs. This year's team have the talent but hit a road bump recently. They usually play well under pressure, but this year they made some unusual choices in their captains and that, plus the loss of some key players, set off a chain reaction that culminated in some losses and a serious beating where I saw them emotionally unravel. They are burdened with team history and are finding it difficult to handle the pressure.

The team were clearly struggling to repeat success and were suffering from the attitude killers of high expectations and the heavy consequences of defeat. The programme Coach Kerri and I agreed was based on rebuilding passion, self-esteem, team identity and competitive toughness:

- Making soccer fun again
- Increasing communication to decrease anxiety
- Rebuilding team identity and visualising what could be:
  - The great feeling of being part of a team and family
  - Deciding what is special about this team
- Adding some social events to reconnect everybody
- Setting new goals and team expectations:
  - Focusing on performance goals—'This is the way we want to play'
  - Ignoring outcome goals—'Let the score take care of itself'
- Reestablishing good practice habits and ensuring role clarity so that the players know what they are supposed to do in every situation in the field
- Having each player declare to her teammates,
  - 'These are the three things I will do well for the team . . .' and
  - 'This is how I will be a good team member . . .'
- Discussing and coming to terms with failure and removing fear
  - Reminding players that failure is a learning moment
  - Asking players, 'What is the worst that can happen?'
- Committing to continual improvement
- Gradually increasing the team's challenges as confidence is rebooted

The skill of the coach in applying the programme gradually turned the team around. The key, however, was when Kerri offset the power of the captains by asking for leadership from everybody in the team. Two of the younger, talented players came out of their shells, and suddenly the team had inspirational leadership. The team responded, regained their hunger and competitive fire and rebuilt their winning record the next season!

REFERENCES

Agassi, A. 2009. *Open—An Autobiography*. London: Harper Collins.

Anderson, D. 2001. *No-Nonsense Leadership*. Agoura Hills, CA, USA: Anderson.

Beswick, B. 2010. *Focused for Soccer, Second Edition*. Champaign, IL: Human Kinetics.

Billick, B., with Peterson, J.A. 2001. *Competitive Leadership: Twelve Principles for Success*. Chicago: Triumph.

Carroll, P. 2010. *Win Forever*. New York: Penguin.

Championship Performance. July 2014, Vol 18 Issue 213, p6

Cohn, P., quoted in Brady, E. 2008 *Sports World's Great Collapses Tied to Pressure, Momentum*. 16 September. Published online in *USA Today*. USAToday.com.

Colvin, G. 2008. *Talent Is Overrated*. London: Nicholas Brealey.

Crothers, T. 2006. *The Man Watching*. Ann Arbor, MI, USA: Sports Media Group.

Dorrance, A., and Nash, T. 2014 *Training Soccer Champions*. Brattleboro, VT, USA: Echo Point Books and Media.

Dweck, C. 2006. *Mindset—the New Psychology of Success*. New York: Random House.

Edwards, L. 2013. All Hail Paolo Di Canio, the New Emperor of Sunderland. *Daily Telegraph*, 22 April, p S10.

Edwards, L. 2014. Newcastle Manager Alan Pardew Admires Southampton Academy and Says Middle-Class Players Lead the Way. *Daily Telegraph*, 28 March, p 13.

Elberse, A., and Ferguson, A. 2013. Ferguson's Formula. *Harvard Business Review* 91 (10), 116–125.

Giacobbi, P.R., Lynn, T.R., Wetherington, J.M. 2004. Stress and Coping During the Transition to University for First Year Female Athletes. *Sports Psychologist* 18 (1), 1–20.

Gibson, C., Pratt, M., Roberts, K., Weynes, E. 2001. *Peak Performance*. London: Profile Books.

Gladwell, M. 2000. *The Tipping Point*. New York: Little, Brown.

Goleman, D. 1995. *Emotional Intelligence*. New York: Bantam Books.

Gordon, J. 2007. *The Energy Bus*. Hoboken, NJ, USA: Wiley.

Grover, T.S. 2013. *Relentless—From Good to Great to Unstoppable*. New York: Simon and Schuster.

Harker, G. 2014. *Leadership Intelligence. Business and Economics Leadership*. Printed in Germany by Amazon Distribution.

Hawkey, I. 2005. Are They Keane II? *Sunday Times*, 2 October 2005.

Holley, M. 2011. *War Room*. New York: Harper Collins.

Holtz, L. 1999. *Winning Every Day*. New York: Harper Collins.

Howard, P. 2014. Gerard Piqué: Manchester City Shouldn't Get too Hung Up on Lionel Messi, Neymar and Pedro Can Do the Damage. *Daily Telegraph*, 15 February, p S13.

Hughes, M. 2008. 'We Lacked Stomach for Fight,' Says John Terry. *The Times*, 6 November.

Hughes, M. 2015. 'Obsessive Desire to Win has made Mourinho the Best,' Says Fabregas. *The Times*, 5 May, p 64.

Jackson, P. 2013. *Eleven Rings—the Soul of Success*. New York: Penguin Press.

Kanter, R.M. 2004. *Confidence*. New York: Three Rivers Press.

Keown, M. 2014. David Moyes Couldn't Find a Settled Side and Picked 51 Different Starting XIs in 51 Games! *Daily Mail*, 22 April, p 66.

Kerr, J. 2013. *Legacy—15 Lessons in Leadership.* London: Constable.

Krag, M. 2012, 18 October. bundesligafanatic.com.

Lavin, J. 2005. *Management Secrets of the New England Patriots* (Vol 1). Stamford, CT, USA: Pointer Press.

Lavin, J. 2005. *Management Secrets of the New England Patriots* (Vol 2). Stamford, CT, USA: Pointer Press.

Lewis, R. 2007. *A Review of Young Player Development in Professional Football.* http://assets.ngin.com/attachments/document/0001/3697/ReviewofYoungPlayerDevelopment1_1_.pdf.

Loehr, J.E. 1994. *The New Toughness Training for Sports.* New York: Plume.

Loehr, J., and Schwartz, T. 2003. *On Form—the Power of Full Engagement.* London: Nicholas Brealey.

Maister, D., Green, C., and Galford, R. 2002. *The Trusted Advisor.* London: Simon & Schuster.

Newman, M. 2007. *Emotional Capitalists.* Hoboken, NJ, USA: Wiley.

Northcroft, J. 2011. Stick Around—You Might Win Something, *Sunday Times*, 27 March.

Oxford Dictionary of Sports Science and Medicine. 3rd ed. 2006. Oxford: Oxford University Press.

Reng, R. 2011. *A Life Too Short.* London: Random House UK.

Russell, B., and Branch T. 1980. *Second Wind*: *The Memoirs of an Opinionated Man.* New York: Ballantine Books.

Schinke, R.J., Peterson, C., and Couture, R. 2004. A Protocol for Teaching Resilience to High Performance Athletes. Published online in *Journal of Excellence*. Issue no 9. zoneofexcellence.com.

Seligman, M.E.P. 1998. *Learned Optimism.* New York: Pocket Books.

Seligman, M.E.P. 2011. *Flourish.* London: Nicholas Brealey.

Selk, J. 2009. *10 Minute Toughness.* New York: McGraw-Hill

Thompson, J. 1995. *Positive Coaching*: *Building Character and Self-Esteem Through Sports.* Portola Valley, CA, USA: Warde.

Thompson, J. 2003. *The Double-Goal Coach.* New York: Harper Collins.

Walsh, B., Billick, B., and Peterson, J. 1998. *Finding the Winning Edge.* Champaign, IL, USA: Sports Publishing.

Walsh, B. 2009. *The Score Takes Care of Itself*: *My Philosophy of Leadership.* New York: Penguin Books.

Wilson, J. 2011a. Arsenal V Barcelona: Champions League Contest Will Be A Clash of Shared Ideals and Principles. *Daily Telegraph*, 14 February, p 57.

Wilson, J. 2011b. Arsene Wenger Calls on Arsenal to Show More Mental Strength in the Race for the Premier League Title. *Daily Telegraph*, 1 January, p 56.

Wilson, J, 2014a. Miroslav Klose Hails Germany's Perfect 'Super Blend' After Becoming World Cup's Record Goalscorer. *Daily Telegraph*, 9 July, p S6.

Wilson, J. 2014b. Mario Gotze Was Told by Joachim Low to Show the World 'He Is Better Than Lionel Messi', *Daily Telegraph*, 14 July, p S5.

Wilson, J. 2014c. Chelsea Manager Jose Mourinho Hits Back at Eden Hazard in Tactics Row, *Daily Telegraph*, 2 May, p S2.

Winter, H. 2014. World Cup 2014: FIFA Study Explains Why This Is Officially One of the Greatest Tournaments of All. *Daily Telegraph*, 3 July, p S10.

Yukelson, D., Rose, R. 2014. *The Psychology of Ongoing Excellence—an NCAA Coach's Perspective on Winning Multiple National Championships. Journal of Sport Psychology in Action*, no 5, 44–58.

INDEX

Note: The fully italicized *See references* refer to a type of heading rather than to specific headings.
Note: The italicized *f* and *t* following page numbers refer to figures and tables, respectively.

ABOUT THE AUTHOR

Bill Beswick is a leader in the field of applied sport psychology, internationally renowned for his work with elite soccer players and teams. After earning a master's degree he worked as head coach of England's gold-medal-winning basketball team at the Commonwealth Games. Beswick became the first full-time performance psychologist in English professional soccer.

Beswick has worked at Manchester United, Middlesbrough and Sunderland in the English Premier League and FC Twente in the Dutch Eredivisie. He has been a contributor to UEFA Pro Licence award courses for European football associations. He has international experience with the England U18 and U21 squads and as team psychologist with the English senior men's national team. He is currently a consulting performance psychologist with Derby County FC in the English Championship Division, the English men's rugby team and the British Olympic swimming team, along with advising athletic programs in the United States, including the one at Clemson University.

Beswick's book *Focused for Soccer* (Human Kinetics, 2010) is now in its second edition and is regarded as one of the best guides ever on psychology of performance in the sport.